COLLECTED POEMS

COLLECTED POEMS

(1914–1947)

ROBERT GRAVES

CASSELL

AND COMPANY LIMITED

LONDON, TORONTO, MELBOURNE AND SYDNEY

First published 1948

Printed in Great Britain
by T. and A. CONSTABLE LTD., Hopetoun Street,
Printers to the University of Edinburgh
F. 747

CONTENTS

II

III

IV

V

VI

FOREWORD

IN Egypt in 1926 I collected all the poems I had
published during the previous twelve years, discarded
most of them, revised and republished the remainder.
Twelve years later with the help of Laura Riding—
we had long been in close literary partnership—I
made a second revision, and a revision of all the
poems that I had written meanwhile. Having by
then a clearer notion of the poetic course that I was
steering I could discard more generously than before,
so that the new book was shorter by forty pages.

Here is a list of the volumes (now all out of print)
that I drew upon:—

Over the Brazier (Poetry Bookshop, 1916). *Goliath
and David* (privately printed, Chiswick Press, 1916).
Fairies and Fusiliers (W. Heinemann, 1917). *The
Treasure Box* (privately printed, Chiswick Press, 1919).
Country Sentiment (Martin Secker, 1920). *The Pier-
Glass* (Martin Secker, 1921). *Whipperginny* (William
Heinemann, 1922). *The Feather Bed* (Hogarth Press,
1923). *Mock Beggar Hall* (Hogarth Press, 1924).
Welchman's Hose (The Fleuron Press, 1925). *The
Marmosite's Miscellany*, by John Doyle (Hogarth
Press, 1925). *Poems: 1914-26* (William Heinemann,
1927). *Poems: 1929* (The Seizin Press, 1929). *Ten
Poems More* (The Hours Press, 1930). *Poems:
1926-30* (William Heinemann, 1930). *To Whom
Else?* (The Seizin Press, 1931). *Poems: 1930-33*

(Arthur Barker, 1933). *Epilogue*, Volumes I, II and III (The Seizin Press and Constable, 1935, 1936, 1937).

Now to make further improvements: the removal of another twenty poems, the revision of several more, the restoration of four early ones from the 1926 edition, and this shortened foreword.

The order is roughly chronological. At the end come forty-four poems from *Poems:* 1938-45 (Cassell, 1946); seventeen more recent ones, including translations of magical texts from the Welsh, Irish and Greek which are discussed in my forthcoming *White Goddess* (Faber & Faber); and a stray poem, *Gulls and Men* (1936), which I left behind in my Majorcan home when I went off in a hurry at the outbreak of the Spanish Civil War, and found waiting for revision on my work-table when I returned ten years later.

R. G.

Deyá, Majorca,
1947.

I

A

IN THE WILDERNESS

He, of his gentleness,
Thirsting and hungering
Walked in the wilderness;
Soft words of grace he spoke
Unto lost desert-folk
That listened wondering.
He heard the bittern call
From ruined palace-wall,
Answered him brotherly;
He held communion
With the she-pelican
Of lonely piety.
Basilisk, cockatrice,
Flocked to his homilies,
With mail of dread device,
With monstrous barbèd stings,
With eager dragon-eyes;
Great bats on leathern wings
And old, blind, broken things
Mean in their miseries.
Then ever with him went,
Of all his wanderings
Comrade, with ragged coat,
Gaunt ribs—poor innocent—
Bleeding foot, burning throat,
The guileless young scapegoat:
For forty nights and days
Followed in Jesus' ways,
Sure guard behind him kept,
Tears like a lover wept.

3

THE HAUNTED HOUSE

'Come, surly fellow, come: a song!'
  What, fools? Sing to you?
Choose from the clouded tales of wrong
  And terror I bring to you:

Of a night so torn with cries,
  Honest men sleeping
Start awake with rabid eyes,
  Bone-chilled, flesh creeping,

Of spirits in the web-hung room
  Up above the stable,
Groans, knockings in the gloom,
  The dancing table,

Of demons in the dry well
  That cheep and mutter,
Clanging of an unseen bell,
  Blood choking the gutter,

Of lust filthy past belief
  Lurking unforgotten,
Unrestrainable endless grief
  In breasts long rotten.

A song? What laughter or what song
  Can this house remember?
Do flowers and butterflies belong
  To a blind December?

REPROACH

Your grieving moonlight face looks down
  Through the forest of my fears,
Crowned with a spiny bramble-crown,
  Bedewed with evening tears.

Why do you say 'untrue, unkind',
  Reproachful eyes vexing my sleep?
I strain in memory, but I find
  No cause why you should weep.

Untrue? But when, what broken oath?
  Unkind? I know not even your name.
Unkind, untrue, you call me both,
  Stabbing my heart with shame.

The black trees shudder, dropping snow,
  The stars tumble and spin.
Speak, speak, or how may a child know
  His ancestral sin?

THE FINDING OF LOVE

Pale at first and cold,
Like wizard's lily-bloom
Conjured from the gloom,
Like torch of glow-worm seen
Through grasses shining green
By children half in fright,
Or Christmas candlelight
Flung on the outer snow,
Or tinsel stars that show
Their evening glory
With sheen of fairy story—

Now with his blaze
Love dries the cobweb maze
Dew-sagged upon the corn,
He brings the flowering thorn,
Mayfly and butterfly,
And pigeons in the sky,
Robin and thrush,
And the long bulrush,
The cherry under the leaf,
Earth in a silken dress,
With end to grief,
With joy in steadfastness.

He fell in victory's fierce pursuit,
   Holed through and through with shot;
A sabre sweep had hacked him deep
   'Twixt neck and shoulder-knot.

The potman cannot well recall,
   The ostler never knew,
Whether that day was Malplaquet,
   The Boyne, or Waterloo.

But there he hangs, a tavern sign,
   With foolish bold regard
For cock and hen and loitering men
   And wagons down the yard.

Raised high above the hayseed world
   He smokes his china pipe;
And now surveys the orchard ways,
   The damsons clustering ripe—

Stares at the churchyard slabs beyond,
   Where country neighbours lie:
Their brief renown set lowly down,
   But his invades the sky.

He grips a tankard of brown ale
   That spills a generous foam:
Often he drinks, they say, and winks
   At drunk men lurching home.

No upstart hero may usurp
  That honoured swinging seat;
His seasons pass with pipe and glass
  Until the tale's complete—

And paint shall keep his buttons bright
  Though all the world's forgot
Whether he died for England's pride
  By battle or by pot.

ROCKY ACRES

This is a wild land, country of my choice,
With harsh craggy mountain, moor ample and bare.
Seldom in these acres is heard any voice
But voice of cold water that runs here and there
Through rocks and lank heather growing without care.
No mice in the heath run, no song-birds fly
For fear of the buzzard that floats in the sky.

He soars and he hovers, rocking on his wings,
He scans his wide parish with a sharp eye,
He catches the trembling of small hidden things,
He tears them in pieces, dropping them from the sky;
Tenderness and pity the heart will deny,
Where life is but nourished by water and rock—
A hardy adventure, full of fear and shock.

Time has never journeyed to this lost land,
Crakeberry and heather bloom out of date,
The rocks jut, the streams flow singing on either hand,
Careless if the season be early or late,
The skies wander overhead, now blue, now slate;
Winter would be known by his cutting snow
If June did not borrow his armour also.

Yet this is my country, beloved by me best,
The first land that rose from Chaos and the Flood,
Nursing no valleys for comfort and rest,
Trampled by no shod hooves, bought with no blood.
Sempiternal country whose hill tops have stood
Stronghold for the proud gods when on earth they go,
Terror for fat burghers on far plains below.

A*   9

OUTLAWS

Owls—they whinny down the night;
  Bats go zigzag by.
Ambushed in shadow beyond sight
  The outlaws lie.

Old gods, tamed to silence, there
  In the wet woods they lurk,
Greedy of human stuff to snare
  In nets of murk.

Look up, else your eye will drown
  In a moving sea of black;
Between the tree-tops, upside down,
  Goes the sky-track.

Look up, else your feet will stray
  Toward that dim ambuscade
Where spider-like they trap their prey
  In webs of shade.

For though creeds whirl away in dust,
  Faith fails and men forget,
These agèd gods of fright and lust
  Cling to life yet—

Old gods almost dead, malign,
  Starved of their ancient dues—
Incense and grain, fire, blood and wine
  And an unclean muse,

10

Banished to woods and a sickly moon,
   Shrunk to mere bogey things,
Who spoke with thunder once at noon
   To prostrate kings,

With thunder from an open sky
   To warrior, tyrant, priest,
Bowing in fear with a dazzled eye
   Toward the dread East—

Proud gods, humbled, sunk so low,
   Living with ghosts and ghouls,
And ghosts of ghosts and last year's snow
   And dead toadstools.

ONE HARD LOOK

Small gnats that fly
In hot July
And lodge in sleeping ears
Can rouse therein
A trumpet's din
With Day of Judgement fears.

Small mice at night
Can wake more fright
Than lions at midday;
A straw can crack
The camel's back—
There is no easier way.

One smile relieves
A heart that grieves
Though deadly sad it be,
And one hard look
Can close the book
That lovers love to see.

A FROSTY NIGHT

'Alice, dear, what ails you,
  Dazed and lost and shaken?
Has the chill night numbed you?
  Is it fright you have taken?'

'Mother, I am very well,
  I was never better.
Mother, do not hold me so,
  Let me write my letter.'

'Sweet, my dear, what ails you?'
  'No, but I am well.
The night was cold and frosty—
  There's no more to tell.'

'Ay, the night was frosty,
  Coldly gaped the moon,
Yet the birds seemed twittering
  Through green boughs of June.

'Soft and thick the snow lay,
  Stars danced in the sky—
Not all the lambs of May-day
  Skip so bold and high.

'Your feet were dancing, Alice,
  Seemed to dance on air,
You looked a ghost or angel
  In the star-light there.

'Your eyes were frosted star-light;
  Your heart, fire and snow.
Who was it said, "I love you"?'
  'Mother, let me go!'

ALLIE

Allie, call the birds in,
  The birds from the sky!
Allie calls, Allie sings,
  Down they all fly:
First there came
Two white doves,
  Then a sparrow from his nest,
Then a clucking bantam hen,
  Then a robin red-breast.

Allie, call the beasts in,
  The beasts, every one!
Allie calls, Allie sings,
  In they all run:
First there came
Two black lambs,
  Then a grunting Berkshire sow,
Then a dog without a tail,
  Then a red and white cow.

Allie, call the fish up,
  The fish from the stream!
Allie calls, Allie sings,
  Up they all swim:
First there came
Two gold fish,
  A minnow and a miller's thumb,
Then a school of little trout,
  Then the twisting eels come.

Allie, call the children,
   Call them from the green!
Allie calls, Allie sings,
   Soon they run in:
First there came
Tom and Madge,
   Kate and I who'll not forget
How we played by the water's edge
   Till the April sun set.

Unicorn with bursting heart
  Breath of love has drawn:
On his desolate crags apart,
  At rumour of dawn,

Has blared aloud his pride
  This long age mute,
Lurched his horn from side to side,
  Lunged with his foot.

'Like a storm of sand I run
  Breaking the desert's boundaries,
I go in hiding from the sun
  In thick shade of trees.

'Straight was the track I took
  Across the plains, but here with briar
And mire the tangled alleys crook,
  Baulking desire.

'O there, what glinted white?
  (A bough still shakes.)
What was it darted from my sight
  Through the forest brakes?

'Where are you fled from me?
  I pursue, you fade;
I run, you hide from me
  In the dark glade.

'Towering high the trees grow,
  The grass grows thick.
Where you are I do not know,
  You run so quick.'

HENRY AND MARY

Henry was a young king,
   Mary was his queen;
He gave her a snowdrop
   On a stalk of green.

Then all for his kindness
   And all for his care
She gave him a new-laid egg
   In the garden there.

'Love, can you sing?'
             'I cannot sing.'
  'Or tell a tale?'
             'Not one I know.'
'Then let us play at queen and king
   As down the garden walks we go.'

LOVE WITHOUT HOPE

Love without hope, as when the young bird-catcher
Swept off his tall hat to the Squire's own daughter,
So let the imprisoned larks escape and fly
Singing about her head, as she rode by.

WHAT DID I DREAM?

What did I dream? I do not know—
    The fragments fly like chaff.
Yet, strange, my mind was tickled so
    I cannot help but laugh.

Pull the curtains close again,
    Tuck me grandly in;
Must a world of humour wane
    Because birds begin

Descanting in a restless tone,
    Rousing me from sleep—
The finest entertainment known,
    And given rag-cheap?

THE COUNTRY DANCE

More slowly the sun travels West,
    Earth warming beneath,
Man's heart swelling tight in his breast
    As a bud in the sheath.

For the tender and unquiet season,
    The Spring, drawing on
Kindles flame in the eye, chokes the reason
    And silvers the swan.

Leap high, jealous Ralph; jet it neat,
    Pretty Jill, and remove
By employment of elbows and feet
    The green sickness of love.

THE TROLL'S NOSEGAY

A simple nosegay! was that much to ask?
(Winter still gloomed, with scarce a bud yet showing).
He loved her ill, if he resigned the task.
'Somewhere,' she cried, 'there must be blossom
　　blowing.'
It seems my lady wept and the troll swore
By Heaven he hated tears: he'd cure her spleen—
Where she had begged one flower he'd shower four-
　　score,
A bunch fit to amaze a China Queen.

Cold fog-drawn Lily, pale mist-magic Rose
He conjured, and in a glassy cauldron set
With elvish unsubstantial Mignonette
And such vague bloom as wandering dreams enclose.
But she?
　　　　Awed,
　　　　　　Charmed to tears,
　　　　　　　　　Distracted,
　　　　　　　　　　　Yet—
Even yet, perhaps, a trifle piqued—who knows?

THE HILLS OF MAY

Walking with a virgin heart
  The green hills of May,
Me, the Wind, she took as lover
  By her side to play,

Let me toss her untied hair,
  Let me shake her gown,
Careless though the daisies redden,
  Though the sun frown,

Scorning in her gay courage
  Lesser love than this,
My cool spiritual embracing,
  My secret kiss.

So she walked, the proud lady,
  So danced or ran,
So she loved with a whole heart,
  Neglecting man. . . .

Fade, fail, innocent stars
  On the green of May:
She has left our bournes for ever,
  Too fine to stay.

LOST LOVE

His eyes are quickened so with grief,
He can watch a grass or leaf
Every instant grow; he can
Clearly through a flint wall see,
Or watch the startled spirit flee
From the throat of a dead man.
    Across two counties he can hear
And catch your words before you speak.
The woodlouse or the maggot's weak
Clamour rings in his sad ear,
And noise so slight it would surpass
Credence—drinking sound of grass,
Worm talk, clashing jaws of moth
Chumbling holes in cloth;
The groan of ants who undertake
Gigantic loads for honour's sake
(Their sinews creak, their breath comes thin);
Whir of spiders when they spin,
And minute whispering, mumbling, sighs
Of idle grubs and flies.
    This man is quickened so with grief,
He wanders god-like or like thief
Inside and out, below, above,
Without relief seeking lost love.

VAIN AND CARELESS

Lady, lovely lady,
  Careless and gay!
Once, when a beggar called,
  She gave her child away.

The beggar took the baby,
  Wrapped it in a shawl—
'Bring him back,' the lady said,
  'Next time you call.'

Hard by lived a vain man,
  So vain and so proud
He would walk on stilts
  To be seen by the crowd,

Up above the chimney pots,
  Tall as a mast—
And all the people ran about
  Shouting till he passed.

'A splendid match surely,'
  Neighbours saw it plain,
'Although she is so careless,
  Although he is so vain.'

But the lady played bobcherry,
  Did not see or care,
As the vain man went by her
  Aloft in the air.

This gentle-born couple
  Lived and died apart—
Water will not mix with oil
  Nor vain with careless heart.

AN ENGLISH WOOD

This valley wood is pledged
To the set shape of things,
And reasonably hedged:
Here are no harpies fledged,
No rocs may clap their wings,
Nor gryphons wave their stings.
Here, poised in quietude,
Calm elementals brood
On the set shape of things:
They fend away alarms
From this green wood.
Here nothing is that harms—
No bulls with lungs of brass,
No toothed or spiny grass,
No tree whose clutching arms
Drink blood when travellers pass,
No mount of glass;
No bardic tongues unfold
Satires or charms.
Only, the lawns are soft,
The tree-stems, grave and old;
Slow branches sway aloft,
The evening air comes cold,
The sunset scatters gold.
Small grasses toss and bend,
Small pathways idly tend
Towards no fearful end.

THE BEDPOST

Sleepy Betsy from her pillow
   Sees the post and ball
Of her sister's wooden bedstead
   Shadowed on the wall.

Now this grave young warrior standing
   With uncovered head
Tells her stories of old battle
   As she lies in bed:

How the Emperor and the Farmer,
   Fighting knee to knee,
Broke their swords but whirled their scabbards
   Till they gained the sea.

How the ruler of that shore
   Foully broke his oath,
Gave them beds in his sea cave,
   Then stabbed them both.

How the daughters of the Emperor,
   Diving boldly through,
Caught and killed their father's murderer,
   Old Cro-bar-cru.

How the Farmer's sturdy sons
   Fought the Giant Gog,
Threw him into Stony Cataract
   In the land of Og.

26

Will and Abel were their names,
   Though they went by others:
He could tell ten thousand stories
   Of these lusty brothers.

How the Emperor's elder daughter
   Fell in love with Will
And went with him to the Court of Venus
   Over Hoo Hill;

How Gog's wife encountered Abel
   Whom she hated most,
Stole away his arms and helmet,
   Turned him to a post.

As a post he shall stay rooted
   For yet many years,
Until a maiden shall release him
   With pitying tears.

But Betsy likes the bloodier stories,
   Clang and clash of fight,
And Abel wanes with the spent candle—
   'Sweetheart, good-night!'

THE PIER-GLASS

Lost manor where I walk continually
A ghost, though yet in woman's flesh and blood.
Up your broad stairs mounting with outspread
    fingers
And gliding steadfast down your corridors
I come by nightly custom to this room,
And even on sultry afternoons I come
Drawn by a thread of time-sunk memory.

Empty, unless for a huge bed of state
Shrouded with rusty curtains drooped awry
(A puppet theatre where malignant fancy
Peoples the wings with fear).   At my right hand
A ravelled bell-pull hangs in readiness
To summon me from attic glooms above
Service of elder ghosts; here, at my left,
A sullen pier-glass, cracked from side to side,
Scorns to present the face (as do new mirrors)
With a lying flush, but shows it melancholy
And pale, as faces grow that look in mirrors.

Is there no life, nothing but the thin shadow
And blank foreboding, never a wainscot rat
Rasping a crust?   Or at the window-pane
No fly, no bluebottle, no starveling spider?
The windows frame a prospect of cold skies
Half-merged with sea, as at the first creation—
Abstract, confusing welter.   Face about,
Peer rather in the glass once more, take note
Of self, the grey lips and long hair dishevelled,

Sleep-staring eyes. Ah, mirror, for Christ's love
Give me one token that there still abides
Remote—beyond this island mystery,
So be it only this side Hope, somewhere,
In streams, on sun-warm mountain pasturage—
True life, natural breath; not this phantasma.

APPLES AND WATER

Dust in a cloud, blinding weather,
    Drums that rattle and roar!
A mother and daughter stood together
    By their cottage door.

'Mother, the heavens are bright like brass,
    The dust is shaken high,
With labouring breath the soldiers pass,
    Their lips are cracked and dry.

'Mother, I'll throw them apples down,
    I'll fetch them cups of water.'
The mother turned with an angry frown,
    Holding back her daughter.

'But, mother, see, they faint with thirst,
    They march away to war.'
'Ay, daughter, these are not the first
    And there will come yet more.

'There is no water can supply them
    In western streams that flow;
There is no fruit can satisfy them
    On orchard-trees that grow.

'Once in my youth I gave, poor fool,
    A soldier apples and water;
And may I die before you cool
    Such drouth as his, my daughter.'

ANGRY SAMSON

Are they blind, the lords of Gaza
   In their strong towers,
Who declare Samson pillow-smothered
   And stripped of his powers?

O stolid Philistines,
   Stare now in amaze
At my foxes running in your cornfields
   With their tails ablaze,

At swung jaw-bone, at bees swarming
   In the stark lion's hide,
At these, the gates of well-walled Gaza
   A-clank to my stride.

DOWN

Downstairs a clock had chimed, two o'clock only.
Then outside from the hen-roost crowing came.
Why should the shift-wing call against the clock,
Three hours from dawn? Now shutters click and
 knock,
And he remembers a sad superstition
Unfitting for the sick-bed. . . . Turn aside,
Distract, divide, ponder the simple tales
That puzzled childhood; riddles, turn them over—
Half-riddles, answerless, the more intense.
Lost bars of music tinkling with no sense
Recur, drowning uneasy superstition.

Mouth open, he was lying, this sick man,
And sinking all the while; how had he come
To sink? On better nights his dream went flying,
Dipping, sailing the pasture of his sleep,
But now (since clock and cock) had sunk him down
Through mattress, bed, floor, floors beneath, stairs,
 cellars,
Through deep foundations of the manse; still sinking
Through unturned earth. How had he magicked
 space
With inadvertent motion or word uttered
Of too-close-packed intelligence (such there are),
That he should penetrate with sliding ease
Dense earth, compound of ages, granite ribs
And groins? Consider: there was some word
 uttered,
Some abracadabra—then, like a stage-ghost,
Funereally with weeping, down, drowned, lost!

Oh, to be a child once more, sprawling at ease
On smooth turf of a ruined castle court.
Once he had dropped a stone between flat slabs
That masked an ancient well, mysteriously
Plunging his mind down with it. Hear it go
Rattling and rocketing into secret void!
Count slowly: one, two, three! and echoes come
Fainter and fainter, merged in the gradual hum
Of bees and flies; only a thin draught rises
To chill the drowsy air. There he had lain
As if unborn, until life floated back
From the deep waters. Oh, to renew now
That bliss of repossession, kindly sun
Forfeit for ever, and the towering sky.

Falling, falling! Day closed up behind him.
Now stunned by the violent subterrene flow
Of rivers, whirling down to hiss below
On the flame-axis of this terrible earth;
Toppling upon their waterfall, O spirit. . . .

MERMAID, DRAGON, FIEND

In my childhood rumours ran
  Of a world beyond the door—
Terrors to the life of man
  That the highroad held in store.

Of the mermaids' doleful game
  In deep water I heard tell,
Or lofty dragons puffing flame,
  Of the hornèd fiend of Hell.

Tales like these were too absurd
  For my laughter-loving ear:
Soon I mocked at all I heard,
  Though with cause indeed for fear.

Now I know the mermaid kin
  I find them bound by natural laws:
They have neither tail nor fin,
  But are deadlier for that cause.

Dragons have no darting tongues,
  Teeth saw-edged nor rattling scales,
No fire issues from their lungs,
  No black poison from their tails:

For they are creatures of dark air,
  Unsubstantial tossing forms,
Thunderclaps of man's despair
  In mid-whirl of mental storms.

34

And there's a true and only fiend
  Worse than prophets prophesy,
Whose full powers to hurt are screened
  Lest the race of man should die.

Ever in vain will courage plot
  The dragon's death, in coat of proof;
Or love abjure the mermaid grot;
  Or faith denounce the cloven hoof.

Mermaids will not be denied
  The last bubbles of our shame,
The dragon flaunts an unpierced hide,
  The true fiend governs in God's name.

II

IN PROCESSION

Often, half-way to sleep,
Not yet sunken deep—
The sudden moment on me comes
From a mountain shagged and steep,
With terrible roll of dream drums,
Reverberations, cymbals, horns replying.
When with standards flying,
Horsemen in clouds behind,
The coloured pomps unwind,
The Carnival wagons
With their saints and their dragons
On the scroll of my teeming mind:
The Creation and Flood
With our Saviour's Blood
And fat Silenus' flagons,
And every rare beast
From the South and East,
Both greatest and least,
On and on,
In endless, different procession.
I stand at the top rungs
Of a ladder reared in the air,
And I rail in strange tongues,
So the crowds murmur and stare;
Then volleys again the blare
Of horns, and summer flowers
Fly scattering in showers,
And the sun leaps in the sky,
While the drums thumping by
Proclaim me. . . .
     Oh, then, when I wake,

Could I courage take
To renew my speech,
Could I stretch and reach
The flowers and the ripe fruit
Laid out at the ladder's foot,
Could I rip a silken shred
From the banner tossed ahead,
Could I call a double-flam
From the drums, could the goat
Horned with gold, could the ram
With a flank like a barn-door,
The dwarf, the blackamoor,
Could Jonah and the Whale
And the Holy Grail,
The Ape with his platter
Going clitter-clatter,
The Nymphs and the Satyr,
And every marvellous matter
Come before me here,
Standing near and clear—
Could I make it so that you
Might wonder at them too!
—Glories of land and sea,
Of Heaven glittering free,
Castles hugely built in Spain,
Glories of Cockaigne,
Of that spicy kingdom, Cand,
Of the Delectable Land,
Of the Land of Crooked Stiles,
Of the Fortunate Isles,
Of the more than three-score miles
That to Babylon lead
(A pretty city indeed

Built on a four-square plan),
Of the Land of the Gold Man
Whose eager horses whinny
In their cribs of gold,
Of the Land of Whipperginny,
Of the land where none grows old. . . .

But cowardly I tell,
Rather, of the Town of Hell—
A huddle of dirty woes
And houses in fading rows
Straggled through space:
Hell has no market-place,
Nor point where four ways meet,
Nor principal street,
Nor barracks, nor Town Hall,
Nor shops at all,
Nor rest for weary feet,
Nor theatre, square, or park,
Nor lights after dark,
Nor churches, nor inns,
Nor convenience for sins—
Neither ends nor begins,
Rambling, limitless, hated well,
This Town of Hell
Where between sleep and sleep I dwell.

WARNING TO CHILDREN

Children, if you dare to think
Of the greatness, rareness, muchness,
Fewness of this precious only
Endless world in which you say
You live, you think of things like this:
Blocks of slate enclosing dappled
Red and green, enclosing tawny
Yellow nets, enclosing white
And black acres of dominoes,
Where a neat brown paper parcel
Tempts you to untie the string.
In the parcel a small island,
On the island a large tree,
On the tree a husky fruit.
Strip the husk and pare the rind off:
In the centre you will see
Blocks of slate enclosed by dappled
Red and green, enclosed by tawny
Yellow nets, enclosed by white
And black acres of dominoes,
Where the same brown paper parcel—
Children, leave the string untied!
For who dares undo the parcel
Finds himself at once inside it,
On the island, in the fruit,
Blocks of slate about his head,
Finds himself enclosed by dappled
Green and red, enclosed by yellow
Tawny nets, enclosed by black
And white acres of dominoes,
With the same brown paper parcel

Still untied upon his knee.
And, if he then should dare to think
Of the fewness, muchness, rareness,
Greatness of this endless only
Precious world in which he says
He lives—he then unties the string.

ALICE

When that prime heroine of our nation, Alice,
Climbing courageously in through the Palace
Of Looking Glass, found it inhabited
By chessboard personages, white and red,
Involved in never-ending tournament,
She being of a speculative bent
Had long foreshadowed something of the kind,
Asking herself: 'Suppose I stood behind
And viewed the fireplace of Their drawing-room
From hearthrug level, why must I assume
That what I'd see would need to correspond
With what I now see?   And the rooms beyond?'

Proved right, yet not content with what she had done,
Alice decided to enlarge her fun:
She set herself, with truly British pride
In being a pawn and playing for her side,
And simple faith in simple stratagem,
To learn the rules and moves and perfect them.
So prosperously there she settled down
That six moves only and she'd won her crown—
A triumph surely!   But her greater feat
Was rounding these adventures off complete:
Accepting them, when safe returned again,
As queer but true, not only in the main
True, but as true as anything you'd swear to,
The usual three dimensions you are heir to.
For Alice though a child could understand
That neither did this chance-discovered land
Make nohow or contrariwise the clean
Dull round of mid-Victorian routine,

Nor did Victoria's golden rule extend
Beyond the glass: it came to the dead end
Where empty hearses turn about; thereafter
Begins that lubberland of dream and laughter,
The red-and-white-flower-spangled hedge, the grass
Where Apuleius pastured his Gold Ass,
Where young Gargantua made whole holiday . . .
But further from our heroine not to stray,
Let us observe with what uncommon sense—
Though a secure and easy reference
Between Red Queen and Kitten could be found—
She made no false assumption on that ground
(A trap in which the scientist would fall)
That queens and kittens are identical.

RICHARD ROE AND JOHN DOE

Richard Roe wished himself Solomon,
Made cuckold, you should know, by one John Doe:
Solomon's neck was firm enough to bear
Some score of antlers more than Roe could wear.

Richard Roe wished himself Alexander,
Being robbed of house and land by the same hand:
Ten thousand acres or a principal town
Would have cost Alexander scarce a frown.

Richard Roe wished himself Job the prophet,
Sunk past reclaim in stinking rags and shame—
However ill Job's plight, his own was worse:
He knew no God to call on or to curse.

He wished himself Job, Solomon, Alexander,
For patience, wisdom, power to overthrow
Misfortune; but with spirit so unmanned
That most of all he wished himself John Doe.

THE WITCHES' CAULDRON

In sudden cloud, that blotting distance out,
Confused the compass of the traveller's mind,
Biased his course: three times from the hill's crest
Trying to descend but with no track to follow,
Nor visible landmark—three times he had struck
The same sedged pool of steaming desolation,
The same black monolith rearing up before it.
This third time then he stood and recognized
The Witches' Cauldron, only known before
By hearsay, fly-like on whose rim he had crawled
Three times and three times dipped to climb again
Its uncouth sides, so to go crawling on.

By falls of scree, moss-mantled slippery rock,
Wet bracken, drunken gurgling watercourses
He escaped, limping, at last, and broke the circuit—
Travelling down and down; but smooth descent
Interrupted by new lakes and ridges,
Sprawling unmortared walls of boulder granite,
Marshes; one arm hung bruised where he had fallen;
Blood in a sticky trickle smeared his cheek;
Sweat, gathering at his eyebrows, ran full beads
Into his eyes, making them smart and blur.

At last he blundered on some shepherd's hut—
He thought, the hut took pity and appeared—
With mounds of peat and welcome track of wheels
Which he now followed to a broad green road
That ran from right to left; but still at fault
Whether he stood this side or that of the hill,

The mist being still on all, with little pause
He chose the easier way, the downward way.
Legs were dog-tired already, but this road,
Gentle descent with some relief of guidance,
Maintained his shambling five miles to the hour
Coloured with day-dreams. Then a finger-post
Moved through the mist, pointing into his face,
Yet when he stopped to read gave him no comfort.
Seventeen miles to—somewhere, God knows where—
The paint was weathered to a puzzle
Which cold-unfocused eyes could not attempt—
And jerking a derisive thumb behind it
Up a rough stream-wet path: 'The Witches' Cauldron,
One mile.' Only a mile
For two good hours of stumbling steeplechase!
There was a dead snake by some humorous hand
Twined on the pointing finger; far away
A bull roared hoarsely, but all else was mist.

Then anger overcame him. . . .

ANCESTORS

My New Year's drink is mulled to-night
    And hot sweet vapours roofward twine.
The shades cry *Gloria!* with delight
    As down they troop to taste old wine.

They crowd about the crackling fire,
    Impatient as the rites begin;
Mulled porto is their souls' desire—
    Porto well aged with nutmeg in.

'Ha,' cries the first, 'my Alma wine
    Of one-and-seventy years ago!'
The second cheers 'God bless the vine!'
    The third and fourth like cockerels crow:

They crow and clap their arms for wings,
    They have small pride or breeding left—
Two grey-beards, a tall youth who sings,
    A soldier with his cheek-bone cleft.

O Gloria! for each ghostly shape,
    That whiffled like a candle smoke,
Now fixed and ruddy with the grape
    And mirrored at the polished oak.

I watch their brightening boastful eyes,
    I hear the toast their glasses clink:
'May this young man in drink grown wise
    Die, as we also died, in drink!'

Their reedy voices I abhor,
    I am alive at least, and young.
I dash their swill upon the floor:
    Let them lap grovelling, tongue to tongue.

CHILDREN OF DARKNESS

We spurred our parents to the kiss,
Though doubtfully they shrank from this—
Day had no courage to pursue
What lusty dark alone might do:
Then were we joined from their caress
In heat of midnight, one from two.

This night-seed knew no discontent:
In certitude our changings went.
Though there were veils about his face,
With forethought, even in that pent place,
Down toward the light his way we bent
To kingdoms of more ample space.

Is Day prime error, that regret
For Darkness roars unstifled yet?
That in this freedom, by faith won,
Only acts of doubt are done?
That unveiled eyes with tears are wet—
We loathe to gaze upon the sun?

THE COOL WEB

Children are dumb to say how hot the day is,
How hot the scent is of the summer rose,
How dreadful the black wastes of evening sky,
How dreadful the tall soldiers drumming by.

But we have speech, to chill the angry day,
And speech, to dull the rose's cruel scent.
We spell away the overhanging night,
We spell away the soldiers and the fright.

There's a cool web of language winds us in,
Retreat from too much joy or too much fear:
We grow sea-green at last and coldly die
In brininess and volubility.

But if we let our tongues lose self-possession,
Throwing off language and its watery clasp
Before our death, instead of when death comes,
Facing the wide glare of the children's day,
Facing the rose, the dark sky and the drums,
We shall go mad no doubt and die that way.

LOVE IN BARRENNESS

Below the ridge a raven flew
And we heard the lost curlew
Mourning out of sight below.
Mountain tops were touched with snow;
Even the long dividing plain
Showed no wealth of sheep or grain,
But fields of boulders lay like corn
And raven's croak was shepherd's horn
Where slow cloud-shadow strayed across
A pasture of thin heath and moss.

The North Wind rose: I saw him press
With lusty force against your dress,
Moulding your body's inward grace
And streaming off from your set face;
So now no longer flesh and blood
But poised in marble flight you stood.
O wingless Victory, loved of men,
Who could withstand your beauty then?

SONG OF CONTRARIETY

Far away is close at hand,
Close joined is far away,
Love shall come at your command
Yet will not stay.

At summons of your dream-despair
She might not disobey,
But slid close down beside you there,
And complaisant lay.

Yet now her flesh and blood consent
At the prime of day,
Joy and passion both are spent,
Fading clean away.

Is the person empty air,
Is the spectre clay,
That Love, lent substance by despair,
Wanes and leaves you lonely there
On the bridal day?

THE PRESENCE

Why say 'death'? Death is neither harsh nor kind:
Other pleasures or pains could hold the mind
If she were dead. For dead is gone indeed,
Lost beyond recovery and need,
Discarded, ended, rotted underground—
Of whom no personal feature could be found
To stand out from the soft blur evenly spread
On memory, if she were truly dead.

But living still, barred from accustomed use
Of body and dress and motion, with profuse
Reproaches (since this anguish of her grew
Do I still love her as I swear I do?)
She fills the house and garden terribly
With her bewilderment, accusing me,
Till every stone and flower, table and book,
Cries out her name, pierces me with her look,
'You are deaf, listen!
You are blind, see!'
                    How deaf or blind,
When horror of the grave maddens the mind
With those same pangs that lately choked her breath,
Altered her substance, and made sport of death?

THE LAND OF WHIPPERGINNY

Come closer yet, my honeysuckle, my sweetheart Jinny:
  A low sun is gilding the bloom of the wood—
Is it Heaven, is it Hell, or the Land of Whipperginny
  That holds this fairy lustre, not yet understood?

For stern proud psalms from the chapel on the moors
  Waver in the night wind, their firm rhythm broken,
Lugubriously twisted to a howling of whores
  Or lent an airy glory too strange to be spoken.

Soon the Moon will rise, and upon us have pity,
  Drawing us in secret by an ivory gate
To the fruit-plats and fountains of her silver city
  Where lovers need not argue the tokens of fate.

IN NO DIRECTION

To go in no direction
   Surely as carelessly,
Walking on the hills alone,
   I never found easy.

Either I sent leaf or stick
   Twirling in the air,
Whose fall might be prophetic,
   Pointing 'there',

Or in superstition
   Edged somewhat away
From a sure direction,
   Yet could not stray,

Or undertook the climb
   That I had avoided
Directionless some other time,
   Or had not avoided,

Or called as companion
   Some eyeless ghost
And held his no direction
   Till my feet were lost.

THE CASTLE

Walls, mounds, enclosing corrugations
Of darkness, moonlight on dry grass.
Walking this courtyard, sleepless, in fever;
Planning to use—but by definition
There's no way out, no way out—
Rope-ladders, baulks of timber, pulleys,
A rocket whizzing over the walls and moat—
Machines easy to improvise.
       No escape,
No such thing; to dream of new dimensions,
Cheating checkmate by painting the king's robe
So that he slides like a queen;
Or to cry, 'Not true, not true!'
Like a corpse in the cholera-pit
Under a load of corpses;
Or to run the head against these blind walls,
Enter the dungeon, torment the eyes
With apparitions chained two and two,
And go frantic with fear—
To die and wake up sweating in moonlight
In the same courtyard, sleepless as before.

RETURN

The seven years' curse is ended now
That drove me forth from this kind land,
From mulberry-bough and apple-bough
And gummy twigs the west wind shakes,
To drink the brine from crusted lakes
And grit my teeth on sand.

Now for your cold, malicious brain
And most uncharitable, cold heart,
You, too, shall clank the seven years' chain
On sterile ground for all time cursed
With famine's itch and flames of thirst,
The blank sky's counterpart.

The load that from my shoulder slips
Straightway upon your own is tied:
You, too, shall scorch your finger-tips
With scrabbling on the·desert's face
Such thoughts I had of this green place,
Sent scapegoat for your pride.

Here, Robin on a tussock sits,
And Cuckoo with his call of hope
Cuckoos awhile, then off he flits,
While peals of dingle-dongle keep
Troop-discipline among the sheep
That graze across the slope.

A brook from fields of gentle sun,
Through the glade its water heaves,
The falling cone would well-nigh stun
That Squirrel wantonly lets drop
When up he scampers to tree-top
And dives among the green.

But no, I ask a surer peace
Than vengeance on you could provide.
Then fear no ill from my release:
Be off, elude the curse, disgrace
Some other green and happy place—
This world of fools is wide.

LUST IN SONG

The bards falter in shame, their running verse
Stumbles, with marrow-bones the drunken diners
Pelt them for their delay.
It is a something fearful in the song
Plagues them—an unknown grief that like a churl
Goes commonplace in cowskin
And bursts unheralded, crowing and coughing,
An unpilled holly-club twirled in his hand,
Into their many-shielded, samite-curtained,
Jewel-bright hall where twelve kings sit at chess
Over the white-bronze pieces and the gold;
And by a gross enchantment
Flails down the rafters and leads off the queens—
The wild-swan-breasted, the rose-ruddy-cheeked
Raven-haired daughters of their admiration—
To stir his black pots and to bed on straw.

NOBODY

Nobody, ancient mischief, nobody,
Harasses always with an absent body.

Nobody coming up the road, nobody,
Like a tall man in a dark cloak, nobody.

Nobody about the house, nobody,
Like children creeping up the stairs, nobody.

Nobody anywhere in the garden, nobody,
Like a young girl quiet with needlework, nobody.

Nobody coming, nobody, not yet here,
Incessantly welcomed by the wakeful ear.

Until this nobody shall consent to die
Under his curse must everybody lie—

The curse of his envy, of his grief and fright,
Of sudden rape and murder screamed in the night.

WITHOUT PAUSE

Without cause and without
Pause blankness follows, turning
Man once more into
An autumn elm or
Asp in autumn mist,
His arms upraised, no
Heart or head, moreover
Nothing heard but now
This constant dropping always
Of such heavy drops
Distilled on finger-tips
From autumn mist and
Nowhere immanence or end
Or pause or cause,
But all is blankness
Seeming headache, yet not
Headache, yet not heartache:
Wanting heart and head,
The tree man—false,
Because the angry sap
Has faded down again
To tree roots dreading
Cold, and these abandoned
Leaves lie fallen flat
To make mould for
The pretty primroses that
Spring again in Spring
With little faces blank,
And sap again then
Rising proves the pain
Of Spring a fancy

Not attempted, no: so,
Until the frantic trial,
Blankness only made for
Pondering and tears against
That sudden lurch-away.

FULL MOON

As I walked out that sultry night,
  I heard the stroke of one.
The moon, attained to her full height,
  Stood beaming like the sun:
She exorcized the ghostly wheat
To mute assent in love's defeat,
  Whose tryst had now begun.

The fields lay sick beneath my tread,
  A tedious owlet cried,
A nightingale above my head
  With this or that replied—
Like man and wife who nightly keep
Inconsequent debate in sleep
  As they dream side by side.

Your phantom wore the moon's cold mask,
  My phantom wore the same;
Forgetful of the feverish task
  In hope of which they came,
Each image held the other's eyes
And watched a grey distraction rise
  To cloud the eager flame—

To cloud the eager flame of love,
  To fog the shining gate;
They held the tyrannous queen above
  Sole mover of their fate,
They glared as marble statues glare
Across the tessellated stair
  Or down the halls of state.

And now warm earth was Arctic sea,
  Each breath came dagger-keen;
Two bergs of glinting ice were we,
  The broad moon sailed between;
There swam the mermaids, tailed and finned,
And love went by upon the wind
  As though it had not been.

VANITY

Be assured, the Dragon is not dead
But once more from the pools of peace
Shall rear his fabulous green head.

The flowers of innocence shall cease
And like a harp the wind shall roar
And the clouds shake an angry fleece.

'Here, here is certitude,' you swore,
'Below this lightning-blasted tree.
Where once it strikes, it strikes no more.

'Two lovers in one house agree.
The roof is tight, the walls unshaken.
As now, so must it always be.'

Such prophecies of joy awaken
The toad who dreams away the past
Under your hearth-stone, light-forsaken,

Who knows that certitude at last
Must fall away in vanity—
No gate is fast, no door is fast.

That thunder bursts from the blue sky,
That gardens of the mind fall waste,
That fountains of the heart run dry.

PURE DEATH

We looked, we loved, and therewith instantly
Death became terrible to you and me.
By love we disenthralled our natural terror
Of every comfortable philosopher
Or tall, grey doctor of divinity:
Death stood at last in his true rank and order.

It happened soon, so wild of heart were we,
Exchange of gifts grew to a malady:
Their worth rose always higher on each side
Till there seemed nothing but ungivable pride
That yet remained ungiven, and this degree
Called a conclusion not to be denied.

Then we at last bethought ourselves, made shift
And simultaneously this final gift
Gave: each with shaking hands unlocks
The sinister, long, brass-bound coffin-box,
Unwraps pure death, with such bewilderment
As greeted our love's first accomplishment.

SICK LOVE

O Love, be fed with apples while you may,
And feel the sun and go in royal array,
A smiling innocent on the heavenly causeway,

Though in what listening horror for the cry
That soars in outer blackness dismally,
The dumb blind beast, the paranoiac fury:

Be warm, enjoy the season, lift your head,
Exquisite in the pulse of tainted blood,
That shivering glory not to be despised.

Take your delight in momentariness,
Walk between dark and dark—a shining space
With the grave's narrowness, though not its peace.

IT WAS ALL VERY TIDY

When I reached his place,
The grass was smooth,
The wind was delicate,
The wit well timed,
The limbs well formed,
The pictures straight on the wall:
It was all very tidy.

He was cancelling out
The last row of figures,
He had his beard tied up in ribbons,
There was no dust on his shoe,
Everyone nodded:
It was all very tidy.

Music was not playing,
There were no sudden noises,
The sun shone blandly,
The clock ticked:
It was all very tidy.

'Apart from and above all this,'
I reassured myself,
'There is now myself.'
It was all very tidy.

Death did not address me,
He had nearly done:
It was all very tidy.

They asked, did I not think
It was all very tidy?

I could not bring myself
To laugh, or untie
His beard's neat ribbons,
Or jog his elbow,
Or whistle, or sing,
Or make disturbance.
I consented, frozenly,
He was unexceptionable:
It was all very tidy.

III

CALLOW CAPTAIN

The sun beams jovial from an ancient sky,
  Flooding the round hills with heroic spate.
A callow captain, glaring, sword at thigh,
  Trots out his charger through the camp gate.
Soon comes the hour, his marriage hour, and soon
  He fathers children, reigns with ancestors
Who, likewise serving in the wars, won
  For a much-tattered flag renewed honours.

A wind ruffles the book, and he whose name
  Was mine vanishes; all is at an end.
Fortunate soldier: to be spared shame
  Of chapter-years unprofitable to spend,
To ride off into reticence, nor throw
  Before the story-sun a long shadow.

THIEF

To the galleys, thief, and sweat your soul out
With strong tugging under the curled whips,
That there your thievishness may find full play.
Whereas, before, you stole rings, flowers and watches,
Oaths, jests and proverbs,
Yet paid for bed and board like an honest man,
This shall be entire thiefdom: you shall steal
Sleep from chain-galling, diet from sour crusts,
Comradeship from the damned, the ten-year-chained—
And, more than this, the excuse for life itself
From a boat steered toward battles not your own.

SAINT

This Blatant Beast was finally overcome
And in no secret tourney: wit and fashion
Flocked out and for compassion
Wept as the Red Cross Knight pushed the blade home.

The people danced and sang the paeans due,
Roasting whole oxen on the public spit;
Twelve mountain peaks were lit
With bonfires. Yet their hearts were doubt and rue.

Therefore no grave was deep enough to hold
The Beast, who after days came thrusting out,
Wormy from rump to snout,
His yellow cere-cloth patched with the grave's mould.

Nor could sea hold him: anchored with huge rocks,
He swelled and buoyed them up, paddling ashore
As evident as before
With deep-sea ooze and salty creaking bones.

Lime could not burn him, nor the sulphur-fire:
So often as the good Knight bound him there,
With stink of singeing hair
And scorching flesh the corpse rolled from the pyre.

In the city-gutter would the Beast lie
Praising the Knight for all his valorous deeds:
'Ay, on those water-meads
He slew even me. These death-wounds testify.'

The Knight governed that city, a man shamed
And shrunken: for the Beast was over-dead,
With wounds no longer red
But gangrenous and loathsome and inflamed.

Not all the righteous judgements he could utter,
Nor mild laws frame, nor public works repair,
Nor wars wage, in despair,
Could bury that same Beast, crouched in the gutter.

A fresh remembrance-banquet to forestall,
The Knight turned hermit, went without farewell
To a far mountain-cell;
But the Beast followed as his seneschal,

And there drew water for him and hewed wood
With vacant howling laughter; else all day
Noisome with long decay
Sunning himself at the cave's entry stood.

He would bawl to pilgrims for a dole of bread
To feed the sick saint who once vanquished him
With spear so stark and grim;
Would set a pillow of grass beneath his head,
Would fetch him fever-wort from the pool's brim—
And crept into his grave when he was dead.

THE FURIOUS VOYAGE

So, overmasterful, to sea!
But hope no distant view of sail,
No growling ice, nor weed, nor whale,
Nor breakers perilous on the lee.

Though you enlarge your angry mind
Three leagues and more about the ship
And stamp till every puncheon skip,
The wake runs evenly behind.

And it has width enough for you,
This vessel, dead from truck to keel,
With its unmanageable wheel,
Its blank chart and the surly crew,

In ballast only due to fetch
The turning point of wretchedness
On an uncoasted, featureless
And barren ocean of blue stretch.

SONG: LIFT-BOY

Let me tell you the story of how I began:
I began as the knife-boy and ended as the boot-man,
With nothing in my pockets but a jack-knife and a
    button,
With nothing in my pockets but a jack-knife and a
    button,
With nothing in my pockets.

Let me tell you the story of how I went on:
I began as the lift-boy and ended as the lift-man,
With nothing in my pockets but a jack-knife and a
    button,
With nothing in my pockets but a jack-knife and a
    button,
With nothing in my pockets.

I found it very easy to whistle and play
With nothing in my head or my pockets all day,
With nothing in my pockets.

But along came Old Eagle, like Moses or David,
He stopped at the fourth floor and preached me
    Damnation:
'Not a soul shall be savèd, not one shall be savèd.
The whole First Creation shall forfeit salvation:
From knife-boy to lift-boy, from ragged to regal,
Not one shall be savèd, not you, not Old Eagle,
No soul on earth escapeth, even if all repent——'
So I cut the cords of the lift and down we went,
With nothing in our pockets.

THE NEXT TIME

And that inevitable accident
  On the familiar journey—roughly reckoned
By miles and shillings—in a cramped compartment
  Between a first hereafter and a second?

And when we passengers are given two hours,
  The wheels failing once more at Somewhere-
      Nowhere,
To climb out, stretch our legs and pick wild flowers—
  Suppose that this time I elect to stay there?

ULYSSES

To the much-tossed Ulysses, never done
  With woman whether gowned as wife or whore,
Penelope and Circe seemed as one:
She like a whore made his lewd fancies run,
  And wifely she a hero to him bore.

Their counter-changings terrified his way:
  They were the clashing rocks, Symplegades,
Scylla and Charybdis too were they;
Now they were storms frosting the sea with spray
  And now the lotus island's drunken ease.

They multiplied into the Sirens' throng,
  Forewarned by fear of whom he stood bound fast
Hand and foot helpless to the vessel's mast,
Yet would not stop his ears: daring their song
  He groaned and sweated till that shore was past.

One, two and many: flesh had made him blind,
  Flesh had one pleasure only in the act,
Flesh set one purpose only in the mind—
Triumph of flesh and afterwards to find
  Still those same terrors wherewith flesh was racked.

His wiles were witty and his fame far known,
Every king's daughter sought him for her own,
  Yet he was nothing to be won or lost.
  All lands to him were Ithaca: love-tossed
He loathed the fraud, yet would not bed alone.

THE SUCCUBUS

Thus will despair
In ecstasy of nightmare
Fetch you a devil-woman through the air,
  To slide below the sweated sheet
And kiss your lips in answer to your prayer
  And lock her hands with yours and your feet with
    her feet.

Yet why does she
Come never as longed-for beauty
Slender and cool, with limbs lovely to see,
  (The bedside candle guttering high)
And toss her head so the thick curls fall free
  Of nippled breast, firm belly and long, slender
    thigh?

Why with hot face,
With paunched and uddered carcase,
Sudden and greedily does she embrace,
  Gulping away your soul, she lies so close,
Fathering you with brats of her own race?
  Yet is the fancy grosser than your lusts were gross?

TRUDGE, BODY

Trudge, body, and climb, trudge and climb,
But not to stand again on any peak of time:
Trudge, body.

I'll cool you, body, with a hot sun, that draws the sweat,
I'll warm you, body, with ice-water, that stings the
    blood,
I'll enrage you, body, with idleness, to do
And having done to sleep the long night through:
Trudge, body.

But in such cooling or warming, doing or sleeping,
No pause for satisfaction: henceforth you make address
Beyond heat to the heat, beyond cold to the cold,
Beyond enraged idleness to enraged idleness.
Here no more crowns of hope, and none of regret:
Before each sun may rise, you salute it for set.
The hills hang above you, they smile or glare,
But shall have dropped behind before you lord it there.

Trudge, body, and climb, trudge and climb,
But not to stand again on any peak of time:
Trudge, body.

THE CLOCK MAN

The clocks are ticking with good will:
  They make a cheerful sound.
I am that temporizer still
  Who sends their hands around,
By fresh experiments with birth and age
Teasing the times each time to further courage.

You who are grateful for your birth
  To hours that ticked you free
(And gratefully relapse to earth)
  Your thanks are due to me—
Which I accept, inured to shame, and mock
My vows to timelessness, sworn with the clock.

THE READER OVER MY SHOULDER

You reading over my shoulder, peering beneath
My writing arm—I suddenly feel your breath
Hot on my hand or on my nape,
So interrupt my theme, scratching these few
Words on the margin for you, namely you,
Too-human shape fixed in that shape:—

All the saying of things against myself
And for myself I have well done myself.
What now, old enemy, shall you do
But quote and underline, thrusting yourself
Against me, as ambassador of myself,
In damned confusion of myself and you?

For you in strutting, you in sycophancy,
Have played too long this other self of me,
Doubling the part of judge and patron
With that of creaking grind-stone to my wit.
Know me, have done: I am a proud spirit
And you for ever clay. Have done.

GREEN LOVING

Grass-green and aspen-green,
Laurel-green and sea-green,
Fine-emerald-green—
As green commands the variables of green
(The hue
Loyal to beauty below sky seen),
So love my many loves of you.

But clear sky, the clear eye,
Smiling shames
Love to a confusion of muttered names.
True sky was never seen until to-day:
For tinged before with the gross fears of clay
All skies were, or their mildness burned away
By the sun's lubber flames.

'You in woman's beauty
I shall love till I die,
As living green, earthily,
The immortal sky.'
But death so vaunted is death-memory
And makes of all green loving a told story.

Lover, ungreen yourself, let her far glance
Find yours at her own distance.
Too close your eyes before,
And held no more
Than dreaming images of your own substance.

THE LEGS

There was this road,
And it led up-hill,
And it led down-hill,
And round and in and out.

And the traffic was legs,
Legs from the knees down,
Coming and going,
Never pausing.

And the gutters gurgled
With the rain's overflow,
And the sticks on the pavement
Blindly tapped and tapped.

What drew the legs along
Was the never-stopping,
And the senseless, frightening
Fate of being legs.

Legs for the road,
The road for legs,
Resolutely nowhere
In both directions.

My legs at least
Were not in that rout:
On grass by the road-side
Entire I stood,

Watching the unstoppable
Legs go by
With never a stumble
Between step and step.

Though my smile was broad
The legs could not see,
Though my laugh was loud
The legs could not hear.

My head dizzied, then:
I wondered suddenly,
Might I too be a walker
From the knees down?

Gently I touched my shins.
The doubt unchained them:
They had run in twenty puddles
Before I regained them.

GARDENER

Loveliest flowers, though crooked in their border,
And glorious fruit, dangling from ill-pruned boughs—
Be sure the gardener had not eye enough
To wheel a barrow between the broadest gates
Without a clumsy scraping.

Yet none could think it simple awkwardness;
And when he stammered of a garden-guardian,
That the smooth lawns came by angelic favour,
The pinks and pears in spite of his own blunders,
They nudged at this conceit.

Well, he had something, though he called it nothing—
An ass's wit, a hairy-belly shrewdness
That would appraise the intentions of the angel
By the very difference of his own confusion,
And bring the most to pass.

FRONT DOOR SOLILOQUY

'Yet from the antique heights or deeps of what
Or which was grandeur fallen, sprung or what
Or which, beyond doubt I am grandeur's grandson
True to the eagle nose, the pillared neck,
(Missed by the intervening generation)
Whom large hands, long face, and long feet sort out
From which and what, to wear my heels down even,
To be connected with all reigning houses,
Show sixteen quarterings or sixty-four
Or even more, with clear skin and eyes clear
To drive the nails in and not wound the wood,
With lungs and heart sound and with bowels easy,
An angry man, heaving the sacks of grain
From cart to loft and what and what and which
And even thus, and being no Rousseauist,
Nor artists-of-the-world-unite, or which
Or what, never admitting, in effect,
Touch anything my touch does not adorn—
Now then I dung on my grandfather's doorstep,
Which is a reasonable and loving due
To hold no taint of love or vassalage
And understood only by him and me—
But you, you bog-rat-whiskered, you psalm-griddling,
Lame, rotten-livered, which and what canaille,
You, when twin lackeys, with armorial shovels,
Unbolt the bossy gates and bend to the task,
Be off, work out your heads from between the railings,
Lest we unkennel the mastiff and the Dane—
This house is jealous of its nastiness.'

IN BROKEN IMAGES

He is quick, thinking in clear images;
I am slow, thinking in broken images.

He becomes dull, trusting to his clear images;
I become sharp, mistrusting my broken images.

Trusting his images, he assumes their relevance;
Mistrusting my images, I question their relevance.

Assuming their relevance, he assumes the fact;
Questioning their relevance, I question the fact.

When the fact fails him, he questions his senses;
When the fact fails me, I approve my senses.

He continues quick and dull in his clear images;
I continue slow and sharp in my broken images.

He in a new confusion of his understanding;
I in a new understanding of my confusion.

ON RISING EARLY

Rising early and walking in the garden
Before the sun has properly climbed the hill—
His rays warming the roof, not yet the grass
That is white with dew still.

And not enough breeze to eddy a puff of smoke,
And out in the meadows a thick mist lying yet,
And nothing anywhere ill or noticeable—
Thanks indeed for that.

But was there ever a day with wit enough
To be always early, to draw the smoke up straight
Even at three o'clock of an afternoon,
To spare dullness or sweat?

Indeed, many such days I remember
That were dew-white and gracious to the last,
That ruled out meal-times, yet had no more hunger
Than was felt by rising a half-hour before breakfast,
Nor more fatigue—where was it that I went
So unencumbered, with my feet tramping
Like strangers on the past?

FLYING CROOKED

The butterfly, a cabbage-white,
(His honest idiocy of flight)
Will never now, it is too late,
Master the art of flying straight,
Yet has—who knows so well as I?—
A just sense of how not to fly:
He lurches here and here by guess
And God and hope and hopelessness.
Even the aerobatic swift
Has not his flying-crooked gift.

LARGESSE TO THE POOR

I had been God's own time on travel
From stage to stage, guest-house to guest-house,
And at each stage furnished one room
To my own comfort, hoping God knows what,
Most happy when most sure that no condition
Might ever last in God's own time—
Unless to be death-numb, as I would not.

Yet I was always watchful at my choices
To change the bad at least for a no worse,
And I was strict nowhere to stay long.
In turn from each new home passing
I locked the door and pocketed the key,
Leaving behind goods plainly mine
(Should I return to claim them legally)
Of which I kept particular register—
In nightly rooms and chattels of the occasion
I was, to my own grief, a millionaire.

But now at last, out of God's firmament,
To break this endless journey—
Homeless to come where that awaits me
Which in my mind's unwearying discontent
I begged as pilgrim's due—
To fling my keys as largesse to the poor,
The always travel-hungry God-knows-who,
With, 'Let them fatten on my industry
Who find perfection and eternity
In might-be-worse, a roof over the head,
And any half-loaf better than no bread,
For which to thank God on their knees nightly.'

FRAGMENT OF A LOST POEM

O the clear moment, when from the mouth
A word flies, current immediately
Among friends; or when a loving gift astounds
As the identical wish nearest the heart;
Or when a stone, volleyed in sudden danger,
Strikes the rabid beast full on the snout!

Moments in never. . . .

IV

GALATEA AND PYGMALION

Galatea, whom his furious chisel
From Parian stone had by greed enchanted,
Fulfilled, so they say, Pygmalion's longings:
    Stepped from the pedestal on which she stood,
Bare in his bed laid her down, lubricious,
With low responses to his drunken raptures,
    Enroyalled his body with her demon blood.

Alas, Pygmalion had so well plotted
The art-perfection of his woman monster
That schools of eager connoisseurs beset
    Her famous person with perennial suit;
Whom she (a judgement on the jealous artist)
Admitted rankly to a comprehension
    Of themes that crowned her own, not his repute.

THE DEVIL'S ADVICE TO STORY-TELLERS

Lest men suspect your tale to be untrue,
Keep probability—some say—in view.
But my advice to story-tellers is:
Weigh out no gross of probabilities,
Nor yet make diligent transcriptions of
Known instances of virtue, crime or love.
To forge a picture that will pass for true,
Do conscientiously what liars do—
Born liars, not the lesser sort that raid
The mouths of others for their stock-in-trade:
Assemble, first, all casual bits and scraps
That may shake down into a world perhaps;
People this world, by chance created so,
With random persons whom you do not know—
The teashop sort, or travellers in a train
Seen once, guessed idly at, not seen again;
Let the erratic course they steer surprise
Their own and your own and your readers' eyes;
Sigh then, or frown, but leave (as in despair)
Motive and end and moral in the air;
Nice contradiction between fact and fact
Will make the whole read human and exact.

SEA SIDE

Into a gentle wildness and confusion,
Of here and there, of one and everyone,
Of windy sandhills by an unkempt sea,
Came two and two in search of symmetry,
Found symmetry of two in sea and sand,
In left foot, right foot, left hand and right hand.

80363

The beast with two backs is a single beast,
Yet by his love of singleness increased
To two and two and two and two again,
Until, instead of sandhills, there's a plain
Patterned in two and two, by two and two—
And the sea parts in horror at a view
Of rows of houses coupling, back to back,
While love smokes from the common chimney-stack
With two-four-eight-sixteenish single same
Re-registration of the duple name.

WM. BRAZIER

At the end of Tarriers' Lane, which was the street
We children thought the pleasantest in Town
Because of the old elms growing from the pavement
And the crookedness, when the other streets were
    straight,
[They were always at the lamp-post round the corner,
Those pugs and papillons and in-betweens,
Nosing and snuffling for the latest news]
Lived Wm. Brazier, with a gilded sign,
'Practical Chimney Sweep.' He had black hands,
Black face, black clothes, black brushes and white
    teeth;
He jingled round the town in a pony-trap,
And the pony's name was Soot, and Soot was black.
But the brass fittings on the trap, the shafts,
On Soot's black harness, on the black whip-butt,
Twinkled and shone like any Guardsman's buttons.
Wasn't that pretty? And when we children jeered:
'Hello, Wm. Brazier! Dirty-face Wm. Brazier!'
He would crack his whip at us and smile and bellow,
'Hello, my dears!' [If he was drunk, but otherwise:
'Scum off, you damned young milliners' bastards,
    you!']

Let them copy it out on a pink page of their albums,
Carefully leaving out the bracketed lines.
It's an old story—f's for s's—
But good enough for them, the suckers.

WELSH INCIDENT

'But that was nothing to what things came out
From the sea-caves of Criccieth yonder.'
'What were they? Mermaids? dragons? ghosts?'
'Nothing at all of any things like that.'
'What were they, then?'

                 'All sorts of queer things,
Things never seen or heard or written about,
Very strange, un-Welsh, utterly peculiar
Things. Oh, solid enough they seemed to touch,
Had anyone dared it. Marvellous creation,
All various shapes and sizes and no sizes,
All new, each perfectly unlike his neighbour,
Though all came moving slowly out together.'
'Describe just one of them.'

                 'I am unable.'
'What were their colours?'

               'Mostly nameless colours,
Colours you'd like to see; but one was puce
Or perhaps more like crimson, but not purplish.
Some had no colour.'

             'Tell me, had they legs?'
'Not a leg or foot among them that I saw.'
'But did these things come out in any order?
What o'clock was it? What was the day of the
     week?
Who else was present? What was the weather?'
'I was coming to that. It was half-past three
On Easter Tuesday last. The sun was shining.
The Harlech Silver Band played *Marchog Jesu*
On thirty-seven shimmering instruments,
Collecting for Carnarvon's (Fever) Hospital Fund.

The populations of Pwlheli, Criccieth,
Portmadoc, Borth, Tremadoc, Penrhyndeudraeth,
Were all assembled. Criccieth's mayor addressed them
First in good Welsh and then in fluent English,
Twisting his fingers in his chain of office,
Welcoming the things. They came out on the sand,
Not keeping time to the band, moving seaward
Silently at a snail's pace. But at last
The most odd, indescribable thing of all
Which hardly one man there could see for wonder
Did something recognizably a something.'
'Well, what?'
                              'It made a noise.'
                                        'A frightening noise?'
'No, no.'
                    'A musical noise?   A noise of scuffling?'
'No, but a very loud, respectable noise—
Like groaning to oneself on Sunday morning
In Chapel, close before the second psalm.'
'What did the mayor do?'
                                    'I was coming to that.'

VISION IN THE REPAIR-SHOP

Be sure the crash was worse than ever.
In, flying out, collapsed with music;
Out, flying in, roared up in flames.
The blast was non-continuous.
But what matter? The force generated
At every point of impact
Was, you remarked, dispersed for other uses.
In this you saw the well-geared mind
Of the garage-man-in-chief,
Prime corpse of each new speed-track,
Who by unequalled salesmanship
Engines a car for every son and daughter
In a city of twelve millions—
What prettier traffic-block imaginable
Lasting, day in, day out, for centuries,
While life flows easily down the gutters
Or swings in the air on ropes,
And you and I, stuffing this cotton-wool
Closer into our ears, from habit,
Lie in plaster of Paris on our backs
And drink the drip of many radiators?

INTERRUPTION

If ever against this easy blue and silver
Hazed-over countryside of thoughtfulness,
Far behind in the mind and above,
Boots from before and below approach tramping,
Watch how their premonition will display
A forward countryside, low in the distance—
A picture-postcard square of June grass;
Will warm a summer season, trim the hedges,
Cast the river about on either flank,
Start the late cuckoo emptily calling,
Invent a rambling tale of moles and voles,
Furnish a path with stiles.
Watch how the field will broaden, the feet nearing,
Sprout with great dandelions and buttercups,
Widen and heighten. The blue and silver
Fogs at the border of this all-grass.
Interruption looms gigantified,
Lurches against, treads thundering through,
Blots the landscape, scatters all,
Roars and rumbles like a dark tunnel,
Is gone.   The picture-postcard grass and trees
Swim back to central: it is a large patch,
It is a modest, failing patch of green,
The postage-stamp of its departure,
Clouded with blue and silver, closing in now
To a plain countryside of less and less,
Unpeopled and unfeatured blue and silver,
Before, behind, above.

104

You call the old nurse and the little page
To act survivors on your tragic stage—
You love the intrusive extra character.
'But where's the tragedy,' you say, 'should none
Remain to moralize on what's been done?
Such silence trembles with a sort of laughter.
Tears purge the soul: the nurse's broken line
"O mistress, pretty one, dead!" the page's whine
"Thou too? Alas, fond master!"'

No purge for my disgusted soul, no tears
Will wash away my bile of tragic years,
No sighs vicariously abate my rancour—
If nurse and page survive, I'd have them own
Small sorrow to be left up-stage alone,
And on the bloodiest field of massacre
Either rant out the anti-climax thus:
"'A's dead, the bitch!' 'So's Oscar! Joy for us!
Then fall to rifling pocket, belt and purse
With corky jokes and pantomime of sin;
Or let the feud rage on, page against nurse—
His jewelled dirk, her thundrous rolling-pin.

MIDWAY

Man is the vavasour of this Creation:
Between insufferable monstrosities
And exiguities insufferable,
Midway is his station. We no longer
Need either hang our heads or lift them high
But for the fortunes of finance or love.
We have no truck either with the forebeings
Of Betelgeux or with the atom's git.
Our world steadies: untrembling we renew
Old fears of earthquakes, adders, floods, mad dogs
And all such wholesomes. Nothing that we do
Concerns the infinities of either scale.
Clocks tick with our consent to our time-tables,
Trains run between our buffers. Time and Space
Amuse us merely with their rough-house turn,
Their hard head-on collision in the tunnel.
A dying superstition smiles and hums
'Abide with me'—God's evening prayer, not ours.
So history still is written and is read:
The eternities of divine commonplace.

HELL

Husks, rags and bones, waste-paper, excrement,
   Denied a soul whether for good or evil
And casually consigned to unfulfilment,
   Are pronged into his bag by the great-devil.

Or words repeated, over and over and over,
   Until their sense sickens and all but dies,
These the same fellow like a ghoulish lover
   Will lay his hands upon and hypnotize.

From husks and rags and waste and excrement
   He forms the pavement-feet and the lift-faces;
He leads the sick words into parliament
   To rule a dust-bin world with deep-sleep phrases.

When healthy words or people chance to dine
   Together in this rarely actual scene,
There is a love-taste in the bread and wine,
   Nor is it asked: 'Do you mean what you mean?'

But to their table-converse boldly comes
   The same great-devil with his brush and tray,
To conjure plump loaves from the scattered crumbs,
   And feed his false five thousand day by day.

LEDA

Heart, with what lonely fears you ached,
  How lecherously mused upon
That horror with which Leda quaked
  Under the spread wings of the swan.

Then soon your mad religious smile
  Made taut the belly, arched the breast,
And there beneath your god awhile
  You strained and gulped your beastliest.

Pregnant you are, as Leda was,
  Of bawdry, murder and deceit;
Perpetuating night because
  The after-languors hang so sweet.

SYNTHETIC SUCH

'The sum of all the parts of Such—
   Of each laboratory scene—
Is Such.' While Science means this much
   And means no more, why, let it mean!

But were the science-men to find
   Some animating principle
Which gave synthetic Such a mind
   Vital, though metaphysical—

To such, such an event, I think
   Would cause unscientific pain:
Science, appalled by thought, would shrink
   To its component parts again.

THE FLORIST ROSE

This wax-mannequin nude, the florist rose,
She of the long stem and too glossy leaf,
Is dead to honest greenfly and leaf-cutter:
Behind plate-glass watches the yellow fogs.

Claims kin with the robust male aeroplane
Whom eagles hate and phantoms of the air,
Who has no legend, as she breaks from legend—
From fellowship with sword and sail and crown.

Experiment's flower, scentless (he its bird);
Is dewed by the spray-gun; is tender-thorned;
Pouts, false-virginal, between bud and bloom;
Bought as a love-gift, droops within the day.

LOST ACRES

These acres, always again lost
   By every new ordnance-survey
And searched for at exhausting cost
   Of time and thought, are still away.

They have their paper-substitute—
   Intercalation of an inch
At the so-many-thousandth foot:
   And no one parish feels the pinch.

But lost they are, despite all care,
   And perhaps are likely to be bound
Together in a piece somewhere,
   A plot of undiscovered ground.

Invisible, they have the spite
   To swerve the tautest measuring-chain
And the exact theodolite
   Perched every side of them in vain.

Yet, be assured, we have no need
   To plot such acres of the mind
With prehistoric fern and reed
   And monsters such as heroes find.

Maybe they have their flowers, their birds,
   Their trees behind the phantom fence,
But of a substance without words:
   To walk there would be loss of sense.

AT FIRST SIGHT

'Love at first sight,' some say, misnaming
Discovery of twinned helplessness
Against the huge tug of procreation.

But friendship at first sight? This also
Catches fiercely at the surprised heart
So that the cheek blanches and then blushes.

RECALLING WAR

Entrance and exit wounds are silvered clean,
The track aches only when the rain reminds.
The one-legged man forgets his leg of wood,
The one-armed man his jointed wooden arm.
The blinded man sees with his ears and hands
As much or more than once with both his eyes.
Their war was fought these twenty years ago
And now assumes the nature-look of time,
As when the morning traveller turns and views
His wild night-stumbling carved into a hill.

What, then, was war? No mere discord of flags
But an infection of the common sky
That sagged ominously upon the earth
Even when the season was the airiest May.
Down pressed the sky, and we, oppressed, thrust out
Boastful tongue, clenched fist and valiant yard.
Natural infirmities were out of mode,
For Death was young again: patron alone
Of healthy dying, premature fate-spasm.

Fear made fine bed-fellows. Sick with delight
At life's discovered transitoriness,
Our youth became all-flesh and waived the mind.
Never was such antiqueness of romance,
Such tasty honey oozing from the heart.
And old importances came swimming back—
Wine, meat, log-fires, a roof over the head,
A weapon at the thigh, surgeons at call.
Even there was a use again for God—
A word of rage in lack of meat, wine, fire,
In ache of wounds beyond all surgeoning.

War was return of earth to ugly earth,
War was foundering of sublimities,
Extinction of each happy art and faith
By which the world had still kept head in air,
Protesting logic or protesting love,
Until the unendurable moment struck—
The inward scream, the duty to run mad.

And we recall the merry ways of guns—
Nibbling the walls of factory and church
Like a child, piecrust; felling groves of trees
Like a child, dandelions with a switch!
Machine-guns rattle toy-like from a hill,
Down in a row the brave tin-soldiers fall:
A sight to be recalled in elder days
When learnedly the future we devote
To yet more boastful visions of despair.

DOWN, WANTON, DOWN!

Down, wanton, down! Have you no shame
That at the whisper of Love's name,
Or Beauty's, presto! up you raise
Your angry head and stand at gaze?

Poor bombard-captain, sworn to reach
The ravelin and effect a breach—
Indifferent what you storm or why,
So be that in the breach you die!

Love may be blind, but Love at least
Knows what is man and what mere beast;
Or Beauty wayward, but requires
More delicacy from her squires.

Tell me, my witless, whose one boast
Could be your staunchness at the post,
When were you made a man of parts
To think fine and profess the arts?

Will many-gifted Beauty come
Bowing to your bald rule of thumb,
Or Love swear loyalty to your crown?
Be gone, have done! Down, wanton, down!

A FORMER ATTACHMENT

And glad to find, on again looking at it,
It meant even less to me than I had thought—
You know the ship is moving when you see
The boxes on the quayside sliding away
And growing smaller—and feel a true delight
When the port's cleared and the coast out of sight,
And ships are few, each on its proper course,
With no occasion for approach or discourse.

NATURE'S LINEAMENTS

When mountain rocks and leafy trees
And clouds and things like these,
With edges,

Caricature the human face,
Such scribblings have no grace
Or peace—

The bulbous nose, the sunken chin,
The ragged mouth in grin
Of cretin.

Nature is always so: you find
That all it has of mind
Is wind,

Retching among the empty spaces,
Ruffling the idiot grasses,
The sheep's fleeces.

Whose pleasures are excreting, poking,
Havocking and sucking,
Sleepy licking.

Whose griefs are melancholy,
Whose flowers are oafish,
Whose waters, silly,
Whose birds, raffish,
Whose fish, fish.

TIME

The vague sea thuds against the marble cliffs
And from their fragments age-long grinds
Pebbles like flowers.

Or the vague weather wanders in the fields,
And up spring flowers with coloured buds
Like marble pebbles.

The beauty of the flowers is Time, death-grieved;
The pebbles' beauty too is Time,
Life-wearied.

It is easy to admire a blowing flower
Or a smooth pebble flower-like freaked
By Time and vagueness.

Time is Time's ease and the sweet oil that coaxes
All obstinate locks and rusty hinges
To loving-kindness.

And am I proof against that lovesome pair,
Old age and childhood, twins in Time,
In sorrowful vagueness?

And will I not pretend the accustomed thanks:
Humouring age with filial flowers,
Childhood with pebbles?

THE PHILOSOPHER

Three blank walls, a barred window with no view,
A ceiling within reach of the raised hands,
A floor blank as the walls.

And, ruling out distractions of the body—
Growth of the hair and nails, a prison diet,
Thoughts of escape—

Ruling out memory and fantasy,
The distant tramping of the gaoler's boots,
Visiting mice and such,

What solace here for a laborious mind!
What a redoubtable and single task
One might attempt here:

Threading a logic between wall and wall,
Ceiling and floor, more accurate by far
Than the cob-spider's.

Truth captured without increment of flies—
Spinning and knotting till the cell became
A spacious other head

In which the emancipated reason might
Learn in due time to walk at greater length
And more unanswerably.

ON DWELLING

Courtesies of good-morning and good-evening
From rustic lips fail as the town encroaches:
Soon nothing passes but the cold quick stare
Of eyes that see ghosts, yet too many for fear.

Here I too walk, silent myself, in wonder
At a town not mine though plainly coextensive
With mine, even in days coincident:
In mine I dwell, in theirs like them I haunt.

And the green country, should I turn again there?
My bumpkin neighbours loom even ghostlier:
Like trees they murmur or like blackbirds sing
Courtesies of good-morning and good-evening.

PARENT TO CHILDREN

When you grow up, are no more children,
Nor am I then your parent:
The day of settlement falls.

'Parent', mortality's reminder,
In each son's mouth or daughter's
A word of shame and rage!

I, who begot you, ask no pardon of you;
Nor may the soldier ask
Pardon of the strewn dead.

The procreative act was blind:
It was not you I sired then—
For who sires friends, as you are mine now?

In fear begotten, I begot in fear.
Would you have had me cast fear out
So that you should not be?

OGRES AND PYGMIES

Those famous men of old, the Ogres—
They had long beards and stinking arm-pits,
They were wide-mouthed, long-yarded and great-
    bellied
Yet of no taller stature, Sirs, than you.
They lived on Ogre-Strand, which was no place
But the churl's terror of their vast extent,
Where every foot was three-and-thirty inches
And every penny bought a whole hog.
Now of their company none survive, not one,
The times being, thank God, unfavourable
To all but nightmare shadows of their fame;
Their images stand howling on the hill
(The winds enforced against those wide mouths),
Whose granite haunches country-folk salute
With May Day kisses, and whose knobbed knees.

So many feats they did to admiration:
With their enormous throats they sang louder
Than ten cathedral choirs, with their grand yards
Stormed the most rare and obstinate maidenheads,
With their strong-gutted and capacious bellies
Digested stones and glass like ostriches.
They dug great pits and heaped huge mounds,
Deflected rivers, wrestled with the bear
And hammered judgements for posterity—
For the sweet-cupid-lipped and tassel-yarded
Delicate-stomached dwellers
In Pygmy Alley, where with brooding on them
A foot is shrunk to seven inches
And twelve-pence will not buy a spare rib.

And who would judge between Ogres and Pygmies—
The thundering text, the snivelling commentary—
Reading between such covers he will marvel
How his own members bloat and shrink again.

The Word that in the beginning was the Word
For two or three, but elsewhere spoke unheard,
Found Words to interpret it, which for a season
Prevailed until ruled out by Law and Reason
Which, by a lax interpretation cursed,
In Laws and Reasons logically dispersed;
These, in their turn, found they could do no better
Than fall to Letters and each claim a letter.
In the beginning, then, the Word alone,
But now the various tongue-tied Lexicon
In perfect impotence the day nearing
When every ear shall lose its sense of hearing
And every mind by knowledge be close-shuttered—
But two or three, that hear the Word uttered.

SINGLE FARE

By way of Fishguard, all the lying devils
Are back to Holy Ireland whence they came.
Each took a single fare: which cost them less
And brought us comfort. The dumb devils too
Take single fares, return by rail to Scotland
Whence they came. So the air is cool and easy.
And if, in some quarter of some big city,
A little Eire or a little Scotland
Serves as a rallying-point for a few laggards,
No matter, we are free from taint of them.
And at the fire-side now (drinking our coffee),
If I ask, 'But to what township did they book,
Those dumb devils of Scotland?' you will answer:
'There's the Bass Rock, once more a separate kingdom,
Leagued with Ireland, the same cold grey crag
Screamed against by the gulls that are all devils.'
And of the Irish devils you will answer:
'In Holy Ireland many a country seat
Still stands unburned—as Cooper's Hill, Lisheen,
Cloghan Castle, or Killua in County Galway—
For the devils to enter, unlock the library doors
And write love-letters and long threatening letters
Even to us, if it so pleases them.'

TO WALK ON HILLS

To walk on hills is to employ legs
As porters of the head and heart
Jointly adventuring towards
Perhaps true equanimity.

To walk on hills is to see sights
And hear sounds unfamiliar.
When in wind the pine-tree roars,
When crags with bleating echo,
When water foams below the fall,
Heart records that journey
As memorable indeed;
Head reserves opinion,
Confused by the wind.

A view of three shires and the sea!
Seldom so much at once appears
Of the coloured world, says heart.
Head is glum, says nothing.

Legs become weary, halting
To sprawl in a rock's shelter,
While the sun drowsily blinks
On head at last brought low—
This giddied passenger of legs
That has no word to utter.

Heart does double duty,
As heart, and as head,
With portentous trifling.
A castle, on its crag perched,
Across the miles between is viewed
With awe as across years.

126

Now a daisy pleases,
Pleases and astounds, even,
That on a garden lawn could blow
All summer long with no esteem.

And the buzzard's horrid poise,
And the plover's misery,
And the important beetle's
Blue-green-shiny back. . . .

To walk on hills is to employ legs
To march away and lose the day.
Confess, have you known shepherds?
And are they not a witless race,
Prone to quaint visions?
Not thus from solitude
(Solitude sobers only)
But from long hilltop striding.

TO BRING THE DEAD TO LIFE

To bring the dead to life
Is no great magic.
Few are wholly dead:
Blow on a dead man's embers
And a live flame will start.

Let his forgotten griefs be now,
And now his withered hopes;
Subdue your pen to his handwriting
Until it prove as natural
To sign his name as yours.

Limp as he limped,
Swear by the oaths he swore;
If he wore black, affect the same;
If he had gouty fingers,
Be yours gouty too.

Assemble tokens intimate of him—
A ring, a hood, a chair:
Around these elements then build
A home familiar to
The greedy revenant.

So grant him life, but reckon
That the grave which housed him
May not be empty now:
You in his spotted garments
Shall yourself lie wrapped.

TO EVOKE POSTERITY

To evoke posterity
Is to weep on your own grave,
Ventriloquizing for the unborn:
'Would you were present in flesh, hero,
What wreaths and junketings!'

And the punishment is fixed:
To be found fully ancestral,
To be cast in bronze for a city square,
To dribble green in times of rain
And stain the pedestal.

Spiders in the spread beard;
A life proverbial
On clergy lips a-cackle;
Eponymous institutes,
Their luckless architecture.

Two more dates of life and birth
For the hour of special study
From which all boys and girls of mettle
Twice a week play truant
And worn excuses try.

Alive, you have abhorred
The crowds on holiday
Jostling and whistling—yet you would air
Your death-mask, smoothly lidded,
Along the promenade?

THE POETS

Any honest housewife would sort them out,
Having a nose for fish, an eye for apples.
Is it any mystery who are the sound,
And who the rotten? Never, by her lights.

Any honest housewife who, by ill-fortune,
Ever engaged a slut to scrub for her
Could instantly distinguish from the workers
The lazy, the liars and the petty thieves.

Does this denote a sixth peculiar sense
Gifted to housewives for their vestal needs?
Or is it failure of the usual five
In all unthrifty writers on this head?

DEFEAT OF THE REBELS

The enemy forces are in wild flight.
Poor souls (you say), they were intoxicated
With rhetoric and banners, thought it enough
To believe and to blow trumpets, to wear
That menacing lie in their shakos.

Enough: it falls to us to shoot them down,
The incorrigibles and cowards,
Where they shiver behind rocks, or in ditches
Seek graves that have no headstones to them—
Such prisoners were unprofitable.

Now as our vanguard, pressing on,
Dislodges them from village and town,
Who yelling abandon packs and cloaks,
Their arms and even the day's rations,
We are not abashed by victory,

We raise no pitying monument
To check the counter-stroke of fortune.
These are not spoils: we recognize
Our own strewn gear, that never had been robbed
But for our sloth and hesitancy.

NEVER SUCH LOVE

Twined together and, as is customary,
For words of rapture groping, they
'Never such love,' swore, 'ever before was!'
Contrast with all loves that had failed or staled
Registered their own as love indeed.

And was this not to blab idly
The heart's fated inconstancy?
Better in love to seal the love-sure lips:
For truly love was before words were,
And no word given, no word broken.

When the name 'love' is uttered
(Love, the near-honourable malady
With which in greed and haste they
Each other do infect and curse)
Or, worse, is written down. . . .

Wise after the event, by love withered,
A 'never more!' most frantically
Sorrow and shame would proclaim
Such as, they'd swear, never before were:
True lovers even in this.

THE FALLEN SIGNPOST

The signpost of four arms is down,
But one names your departure-town:
With this for guide you may replant
Your post and choose which road you want—

Logic that only seems obscure
To those deliberately not sure
Whether a journey should begin
With cross-roads or with origin.

The square post, and the socket square—
Now which way round to set it there?
Thus from the problem coaxing out
Four further elements of doubt,

They make the simple cross-roads be
A crux of pure dubiety
Demanding how much more concern
Than to have taken the wrong turn!

THE CHINA PLATE

From a crowded barrow in a street-market
The plate was ransomed for a few coppers,
Was brought gleefully home, given a place
On a commanding shelf.

'Quite a museum-piece,' an expert cries
(Eyeing it through the ready pocket-lens)—
As though a glass case would be less sepulchral
Than the barrow-hearse!

For weeks this plate retells the history
Whenever an eye runs in that direction:
'Near perdition I was, in a street-market
With rags and old shoes.'

'A few coppers'—here once again
The purchaser's proud hand lifts down
The bargain, displays the pot-bank sign
Scrawled raggedly underneath.

Enough, permit the treasure to forget
The emotion of that providential purchase,
Becoming a good citizen of the house
Like its fellow-crockery.

Let it dispense sandwiches at a party
And not be noticed in the drunken buzz,
Or little cakes at afternoon tea
When cakes are in demand.

Let it regain a lost habit of life,
Foreseeing death in honourable breakage
Somewhere between the kitchen and the shelf—
To be sincerely mourned.

CERTAIN MERCIES

Now must all satisfaction
Become mere mitigation
Of an accepted curse?

Must we henceforth be grateful
That the guards, though spiteful,
Are slow of foot and wit?

That by night we may spread
Over the plank bed
A thin coverlet?

That the rusty water
In the unclean pitcher
Our thirst quenches?

That the rotten, detestable
Food is yet eatable
By us ravenous?

That the prison censor
Permits a weekly letter?
(We may write: 'we are well.')

That, with patience and deference,
We do not experience
The punishment cell?

That each new indignity
Defeats only the body,
Pampering the spirit
With obscure, proud merit?

135

THE CUIRASSIERS OF THE FRONTIER

Goths, Vandals, Huns, Isaurian mountaineers,
Made Roman by our Roman sacrament,
We can know little (as we care little)
Of the Metropolis: her candled churches,
Her white-gowned pederastic senators,
The cut-throat factions of her Hippodrome,
The eunuchs of her draped saloons.

Here is the frontier, here our camp and place—
Beans for the pot, fodder for horses,
And Roman arms. Enough. He who among us
At full gallop, the bowstring to his ear,
Lets drive his heavy arrows, to sink
Stinging through Persian corslets damascened,
Then follows with the lance—he has our love.

The Christ bade Holy Peter sheathe his sword,
Being outnumbered by the Temple guard.
And this was prudence, the cause not yet lost
While Peter might persuade the crowd to rescue.
Peter renegued, breaking his sacrament.
With us the penalty is death by stoning,
Not to be made a bishop.

In Peter's Church there is no faith nor truth,
Nor justice anywhere in palace or court.
That we continue watchful on the rampart
Concerns no priest. A gaping silken dragon,
Puffed by the wind, suffices us for God.
We, not the City, are the Empire's soul:
A rotten tree lives only in its rind.

THE LAUREATE

Like a lizard in the sun, though not scuttling
When men approach, this wretch, this thing of rage,
Scowls and sits rhyming in his horny age.

His time and truth he has not bridged to ours,
But shrivelled by long heliotropic idling
He croaks at us his out-of-date humours.

Once long ago here was a poet; who died.
See how remorse twitching his mouth proclaims
It was no natural death, but suicide.

Arrogant, lean, unvenerable, he
Still turns for comfort to the western flames
That glitter a cold span above the sea.

A JEALOUS MAN

To be homeless is a pride
To the jealous man prowling
Hungry down the night lanes,

Who has no steel at his side,
No drink hot in his mouth,
But a mind dream-enlarged,

Who witnesses warfare,
Man with woman, hugely
Raging from hedge to hedge:

The raw knotted oak-club
Clenched in the raw fist,
The ivy-noose well flung,

The thronged din of battle,
Gaspings of the throat-snared,
Snores of the battered dying,

Tall corpses, braced together,
Fallen in clammy furrows,
Male and female,

Or, among haulms of nettle
Humped, in noisome heaps,
Male and female.

He glowers in the choked roadway
Between twin churchyards,
Like a turnip ghost.

(Here, the rain-worn headstone,
There, the Celtic cross
In rank white marble.)

This jealous man is smitten,
His fear-jerked forehead
Sweats a fine musk;

A score of bats bewitched
By the ruttish odour
Swoop singing at his head;

Nuns bricked up alive
Within the neighbouring wall
Wail in cat-like longing.

Crow, cocks, crow loud!
Reprieve the doomed devil,
Has he not died enough?

Now, out of careless sleep,
She wakes and greets him coldly,
The woman at home,

She, with a private wonder
At shoes bemired and bloody—
His war was not hers.

THE CLOAK

Into exile with only a few shirts,
Some gold coin and the necessary papers.
But winds are contrary: the Channel packet
Time after time returns the sea-sick peer
To Sandwich, Deal or Rye. He does not land,
But keeps his cabin; so at last we find him
In humble lodgings at perhaps Dieppe,
His shirts unpacked, his night-cap on a peg,
Passing the day with cards and swordsmanship
Or merry passages with chambermaids,
By night at his old work. And all is well—
The country wine wholesome although so sharp,
And French his second tongue; a faithful valet
Brushes his hat and brings him newspapers.
This nobleman is at home anywhere,
His castle being, the valet says, his title.
The cares of an estate would incommode
Such tasks as now his Lordship has in hand.
His Lordship, says the valet, contemplates
A profitable absence of some years.
Has he no friend at Court to intercede?
He wants none: exile's but another name
For an old habit of non-residence
In all but the recesses of his cloak.
It was this angered a great personage.

THE HALLS OF BEDLAM

Forewarned of madness:
In three days' time at dusk
The fit masters him.

How to endure those days?
(Forewarned is foremad)
'—Normally, normally.'

He will gossip with children,
Argue with elders,
Check the cash account.

'I shall go mad that day—'
The gossip, the argument,
The neat marginal entry.

His case is not uncommon,
The doctors pronounce;
But prescribe no cure.

To be mad is not easy,
Will earn him no money,
But a niche in the news.

Then to-morrow, children,
To-morrow or the next day
He resigns from the firm.

His boyhood's ambition
Was to become an artist—
Like any City man's.

141

To the walls and halls of Bedlam
The artist is welcome—
Bold brush and full palette.

Through the cell's grating
He will watch his children
To and from school.

'Suffer the little children
To come unto me
With their Florentine hair!'

A very special story
For their very special friends—
They burst in the telling:

Of an evil thing, armed,
Tap-tapping on the door,
Tap-tapping on the floor,
'On the third day at dusk.'

Father in his shirt-sleeves
Flourishing a hatchet—
Run, children, run!

No one could stop him,
No one understood;
And in the evening papers. . . .

(Imminent genius,
Troubles at the office,
Normally, normally,
As if already mad.)

OR TO PERISH BEFORE DAY

The pupils of the eye expand
And from near-nothings build up sight;
The pupil of the heart, the ghost,
Swelling parades the dewy land:

With cowardice and with self-esteem
Makes terror in the track that through
The fragrant spotted pasture runs;
And a bird wails across the dream.

Now, if no heavenly window shines
Nor angel-voices cheer the way,
The ghost will overbear the man
And mark his head with fever-signs.

The flowers of dusk that he has pulled
To wonder at when morning's here
Are snail-shells upon straws of grass—
So easily the eye is gulled.

The sounding words that his mouth fill
Upon to-morrow's lip shall droop;
The legs that slide with skating ease
Be stiff to the awakened will.

Or, should he perish before day,
He leaves his lofty ghost behind
Perpetuating uncontrolled
This hour of glory and dismay.

A COUNTRY MANSION

This ancient house so notable
For its gables and great staircase,
Its mulberry-trees and alleys of clipped yew,
Humbles the show of every near domain.

At the beginning it acknowledged owners—
Father, son, grandson—
But then, surviving the last heirs of the line,
Became a place for life-tenancy only.

At the beginning, no hint of fate,
No rats and no hauntings;
In the garden, then, the fruit-trees grew
Slender and similar in long rows.

A bedroom with a low ceiling
Caused little fret at first;
But gradual generations of discomfort
Have bred an anger there to stifle sleep.

And the venerable dining-room,
Where port in Limerick glasses
Glows twice as red reflected
In the memory-mirror of the waxed table—

For a time with paint and flowered paper
A mistress tamed its walls,
But pious antiquarian hands, groping,
Rediscovered the grey panels beneath.

Children love the old house tearfully,
And the parterres, how fertile!
Married couples under the testers hugging
Enjoy an antique bliss as nowhere else.

A smell of mould from loft to cellar,
Yet sap still brisk in the oak
Of the great beams: if ever they use a saw
It will stain, as cutting a branch from a green tree.

. . . Old Parr had lived one hundred years and five
(So to King Charles he bragged)
When he did open penance, in a sheet,
For fornication with posterity.

Old Parr died; not so this mansion
Whose inhabitants, bewitched,
Pour their fresh blood through its historic veins
And, if a tile blow from the roof, tremble.

The last-born of this race of sacristans
Broke the long spell, departed;
They lay his knife and fork at every meal
And every evening warm his bed;

Yet cannot draw him back from the far roads
For trifling by the lily-pool
Or wine at the hushed table where they meet,
The guests of genealogy.

145

It was his childhood's pleasure-ground
And still may claim his corpse,
Yet foster-cradle or foster-grave
He will not count as home.

This rebel does not hate the house,
Nor its dusty joys impugn:
No place less reverend could provoke
So proud an absence from it.

He has that new malaise of time:
Gratitude choking with vexation
That he should opulently inherit
The goods and titles of the extinct.

THE EREMITES

We may well wonder at those bearded hermits
Who like the scorpion and the basilisk
Couched in the desert sands, to undo
Their scurfy flesh with tortures.

They drank from pools fouled by the ass and camel,
Chewed uncooked millet pounded between stones,
Wore but a shame-rag, dusk or dawn,
And rolled in thorny places.

In the wilderness there are no women;
Yet hermits harbour in their shrunken loins
A penitential paradise,
A leaping-house of glory.

Solomons of a thousand lusty love-chants,
These goatish men, burned Aethiopian black,
Kept vigil till the angelic whores
Should lift the latch of pleasure.

And what Atellan orgies of the soul
Were celebrated then among the rocks
They testify themselves in books
That rouse Atellan laughter.

Haled back at last to wear the ring and mitre,
They clipped their beards and, for their stomachs' sake,
Drank now and then a little wine,
And tasted cakes and honey.

147

Observe then how they disciplined the daughters
Of noble widows, who must fast and thirst,
Abjure down-pillows, rouge and curls,
Deform their delicate bodies:

Whose dreams were curiously beset by visions
Of stinking hermits in a wilderness
Pressing unnatural lusts on them
Until they wakened screaming.

Such was the virtue of our pious fathers:
To refine pleasure in the hungry dream.
Pity for them, but pity too for us—
Our beds by their leave lain in.

THE ADVOCATES

Fugitive firs and larches for a moment
Caught, past midnight, by our headlight beam
On that mad journey through unlasting lands
I cannot put a name to, years ago,
(And my companions drowsy-drunk)—these trees
Resume again their sharp appearance, perfect
Of spur and tassel, claiming memory,
Claiming affection: 'Will we be included
In the catalogue? Yes, yes?' they plead.

Green things, you are already there enrolled.
And should a new resentment gnaw in me
Against my dear companions of that journey
(Strangers already then, in thought and deed)
You shall be advocates, charged to deny
That all the good I lived with them is lost.

SELF-PRAISE

No, self-praise does not recommend.
　What shall I do with mine
When so few Englishmen pretend
　Not to be dogs or swine,

That to assume the peacock's part,
　To scream and spread the tail,
Is held a doom-defying art
　And witnesses turn pale?

But praise from fellow-creatures is
　(All Englishmen agree)
The sweetest of experiences
　And confers modesty,

And justifies the silent boast
　Of a bemedalled line:
The most dog-true of dogs, the most
　Egregious swine of swine.

O, let me suffer in self-praise,
　Unfit to occupy
The kennel, for my headstrong ways,
　Too squeamish for the sty.

V

ON PORTENTS

If strange things happen where she is,
So that men say that graves open
And the dead walk, or that futurity
Becomes a womb and the unborn are shed,
Such portents are not to be wondered at,
Being tourbillions in Time made
By the strong pulling of her bladed mind
Through that ever-reluctant element.

THE TERRACED VALLEY

In a deep thought of you and concentration
I came by hazard to a new region:
The unnecessary sun was not there,
The necessary earth lay without care—
For more than sunshine warmed the skin
Of the round world that was turned outside-in.

Calm sea beyond the terraced valley
Without horizon easily was spread,
As it were overhead,
Washing the mountain-spurs behind me:
The unnecessary sky was not there,
Therefore no heights, no deeps, no birds of the air.

Neat outside-inside, neat below-above,
Hermaphrodizing love.
Neat this-way-that-way and without mistake:
On the right hand could slide the left glove.
Neat over-under: the young snake
Through an unyielding shell his path could break.
Singing of kettles, like a singing brook,
Made out-of-doors a fireside nook.

But you, my love, where had you then your station?
Seeing that on this counter-earth together
We went not distant from each other,
I knew you near me in that strange region,
So searched for you, in hope to see you stand
On some near olive-terrace, in the heat,
The left-hand glove drawn on your right hand,
The empty snake's egg perfect at your feet—
154

But found you nowhere in the wide land,
And cried disconsolately, until you spoke
Immediate at my elbow, and your voice broke
This trick of time, changing the world about
To once more inside-in and outside-out.

THE CHALLENGE

In ancient days a glory swelled my thighs,
And sat like fear between my shoulder-blades,
And made the young hair bristle on my poll.

Sun was my crown, green grassflesh my estate,
The wind a courtier, fanning at my cheek,
And plunged I in the stream, its waters hissed.

Queens I had to try my glory on,
And glory-princes my queens bore to me.
Royally I swept off all caitiff crowns.

Were the queens whores? the princes parricides?
Or were the tumbled crowns again worn high?
No, I was king then, if kings ever were.

O cousin princes, glory is hard put by,
And green grassflesh is lovely to a king.
My hawks were lightning darted from my fist.

Time was my chronicler, my deeds age-new,
And death no peril, nor decay of powers.
Glory sat firmly in my body's thrones.

Only, at midnight, rose another crown
That drained the wholesome colour from my realm,
That stilled the wind and froze the headlong stream.

I said: A challenge not to be endured,
A shadow clouding the sweet drunken hour
When with my queens in love I company.

I left the Palace sleeping, I rode out,
I flew my hawk at that thin, mocking crown,
I emptied my full quiver at the sky.

Where went my hawk? He came not home again.
What ailed my horse? He cast me like a sack.
The crown moved ghostly off against the dawn.

And from that hour, though the sun burned as fierce,
Though the wind brought me frequency of spice,
Glory was gone, and numb was all my flesh.

Whose weakling is the vanquished of the Moon?
His own heart's weakling: thievishly he longs
To diadem his head with stolen light.

The Moon's the crown of no high-walled domain
Conquerable by angry reach of pride:
Her icy lands welcome no soldiery.

Thus I was shamed, I wandered in the fields,
I let my nails grow long and my hair long,
Neglecting all the business of my day.

No lovely queen nor wisest minister
Could medicine me out of my wretchedness:
The Palace fell in ruins, the land smoked.

In my lost realm, if grass or flower yet grew,
It sprouted from the shade of broken walls.
I threw the walls flat, crushing flower and grass.

At length in my distemper's latest hour
I rose up shuddering, reckless to live
An idiot pawn of that inhuman power.

Over the mountain peak I watched her glide
And stood dumbfounded by her reasoned look.
With answering reason my sick heart renewed.

So peace fell sudden, and in proof of peace
There sat my flown hawk, hooded on my fist,
And with my knees I gripped my truant horse.

Toward that most clear, unscorching light I spurred.
Whiter and closer shone the increasing disc,
Until it filled the sky, scattering my gaze.

When I might see once more, the day had come
And I was riding through gold harvest-fields,
Toward a rebuilded city, and my home.

Here then in majesty I rule again,
And grassflesh pays me tribute as of old;
In wind and sun and stream my joys I take,
Bounded by white horizons beyond touch.

TO THE SOVEREIGN MUSE

Debating here one night we reckoned that
Between us we knew all the poets
Who bore that sacred name: none bore it clear,
Not one.   Some we commended
For being all they might be in a day
To which poetry was a shrouded emblem,
And some we frowned upon for lawyers' clerks
Drafting conveyances on moral sheepskin,
Or for pantomimists making parody
Of a magnificence they feared to acclaim.

This was to praise you, Sovereign muse,
And to your love our pride devote,
Who pluck the speech-thread from a jargon-tangled
Fleece of a thousand tongues, wills, voices,
To be a single speech, twisted fine;
Snapping it short like Fate then—
'Thus much, no more—'

Thereafter, in acknowledgement of you
We might no longer feign and stutter
As poets of the passionate chance,
Nor claim the indulgence of the hour.
Our tongues must prompter be than those
That wagged with modish lamentation—
Or lost men, otherwise, and renegades
To our confession, maudlin-sane must die
Suicides on the stair of yesterday.

THE AGES OF OATH

To find a garden-tulip growing
Among wild primroses of a wild field,
Or a cuckoo's egg in a blackbird's nest,
Or a giant mushroom, a whole basketful—
The memorable feats of childhood!
Once, by the earthworks, scratching in the soil,
My stick turned up a Roman amber bead. . . .

The lost, the freakish, the unspelt
Drew me: for simple sights I had no eye.
And did I swear allegiance then
To wildness, not (as I thought) to truth—
Become a virtuoso, and this also,
Later, of simple sights, when tiring
Of unicorn and upas?

Did I forget how to greet plainly
The especial sight, how to know deeply
The pleasure shared by upright hearts?
And is this to begin afresh, with oaths
On the true book, in the true name,
Now stammering out my praise of you,
Like a boy owning his first love?

NEW LEGENDS

Content in you,
Andromeda serene,
Mistress of air and ocean
And every fiery dragon,
Chained to no cliff,
Asking no rescue of me.

Content in you,
Mad Atalanta,
Stooping unpausing,
Ever ahead,
Acquitting me of rivalry.

Content in you
Who made King Proteus marvel,
Showing him singleness
Past all variety.

Content in you,
Niobe of no children,
Nor of calamity.

Content in you,
Helen, foiler of beauty.

LIKE SNOW

She, then, like snow in a dark night,
Fell secretly.   And the world waked
With dazzling of the drowsy eye,
So that some muttered 'Too much light,'
And drew the curtains close.
Like snow, warmer than fingers feared,
And to soil friendly;
Holding the histories of the night
In yet unmelted tracks.

THE CLIMATE OF THOUGHT

The climate of thought has seldom been described.
It is no terror of Caucasian frost,
Nor yet that brooding Hindu heat
For which a loin-rag and a dish of rice
Suffice until the pestilent monsoon.
But, without winter, blood would run too thin;
Or, without summer, fires would burn too long.
In thought the seasons run concurrently.

Thought has a sea to gaze, not voyage on;
And hills, to rough the edge of the bland sky,
Not to be climbed in search of blander prospect;
Few birds, sufficient for such caterpillars
As are not fated to turn butterflies;
Few butterflies, sufficient for the flowers
That are the luxury of a full orchard;
Wind, sometimes, in the evening chimneys; rain
On the early morning roof, on sleepy sight;
Snow streaked upon the hilltop, feeding
The fond brook at the valley-head
That greens the valley and that parts the lips;
The sun, simple, like a country neighbour;
The moon, grand, not fanciful with clouds.

END OF PLAY

We have reached the end of pastime, for always,
Ourselves and everyone, though few confess it
Or see the sky other than, as of old,
A foolish smiling Mary-mantle blue;

Though life may still seem to dawdle golden
In some June landscape among giant flowers,
The grass to shine as cruelly green as ever,
Faith to descend in a chariot from the sky—

May seem only: a mirror and an echo
Mediate henceforth with vision and sound.
The cry of faith, no longer mettlesome,
Sounds as a blind man's pitiful plea of 'blind'.

We have at last ceased idling, which to regret
Were as shallow as to ask our milk-teeth back;
As many forthwith do, and on their knees
Call lugubriously upon chaste Christ.

We tell no lies now, at last cannot be
The rogues we were—so evilly linked in sense
With what we scrutinized that lion or tiger
Could leap from every copse, strike and devour us.

No more shall love in hypocritic pomp
Conduct its innocents through a dance of shame,
From timid touching of gloved fingers
To frantic laceration of naked breasts.

Yet love survives, the word carved on a sill
Under antique dread of the headsman's axe;
It is the echoing mind, as in the mirror
We stare on our dazed trunks at the block kneeling.

THE FALLEN TOWER OF SILOAM

Should the building totter, run for an archway!
We were there already—already the collapse
Powdered the air with chalk, and shrieking
Of old men crushed under the fallen beams
Dwindled to comic yelps.   How not terrible
When the event outran the alarm
And suddenly we were free—

Free to forget how grim it stood,
That tower, and what wide fissures ran
Up the west wall, how rotten the under-pinning
At the south-eastern angle.   Satire
Had whirled a gentle wind around it,
As if to buttress the worn masonry;
Yet we, waiting, had abstained from satire.

It behoved us, indeed, as poets
To be silent in Siloam, to foretell
No visible calamity.   Though kings
Were crowned and gold coin minted still and horses
Still munched at nose-bags in the public streets,
All such sad emblems were to be condoned:
An old wives' tale, not ours.

THE GREAT-GRANDMOTHER

That aged woman with the bass voice
And yellowing white hair: believe her.
Though to your grandfather, her son, she lied
And to your father disingenuously
Told half the tale as the whole,
Yet she was honest with herself,
Knew disclosure was not yet due,
Knows it is due now.

She will conceal nothing of consequence
From you, her great-grandchildren
(So distant the relationship,
So near her term),
Will tell you frankly, she has waited
Only for your sincere indifference
To exorcize that filial regard
Which has estranged her, seventy years,
From the folk of her house.

Confessions of old distaste
For music, sighs and roses—
Their false-innocence assaulting her,
Breaching her hard heart;
Of the pleasures of a full purse,
Of clean brass and clean linen,
Of being alone at last;
Disgust with the ailing poor
To whom she was bountiful;
How the prattle of young children
Vexed more than if they whined;
How she preferred cats.

She will say, yes, she acted well,
Took such pride in the art
That none of them suspected, even,
Her wrathful irony
In doing what they asked
Better than they could ask it . . .
But, ah, how grudgingly her will returned
After the severance of each navel-cord,
And fled how far again,
When again she was kind!

She has outlasted all man-uses,
As was her first resolve:
Happy and idle like a port
After the sea's recession,
She does not misconceive the nature
Of shipmen or of ships.
Hear her, therefore, as the latest voice;
The intervening generations (drifting
On tides of fancy still), ignore.

NO MORE GHOSTS

The patriarchal bed with four posts
Which was a harbourage of ghosts
Is hauled out from the attic glooms
And cut to wholesome furniture for wholesome rooms;

Where they (the ghosts) confused, abused, thinned,
Forgetful how they sighed and sinned,
Cannot disturb our ordered ease
Except as summer dust tickles the nose to sneeze.

We are restored to simple days, are free
From cramps of dark necessity,
And one another recognize
By an immediate love that signals at our eyes.

No new ghost can appear. Their poor cause
Was that time freezes, and time thaws;
But here only such loves can last
As do not ride upon the weathers of the past.

VI

A LOVE STORY

The full moon easterly rising, furious,
Against a winter sky ragged with red;
The hedges high in snow, and owls raving—
Solemnities not easy to withstand:
A shiver wakes the spine.

In boyhood, having encountered the scene,
I suffered horror: I fetched the moon home,
With owls and snow, to nurse in my head
Throughout the trials of a new spring,
Famine unassuaged.

But fell in love, and made a lodgement
Of love on those chill ramparts.
Her image was my ensign: snows melted,
Hedges sprouted, the moon tenderly shone,
The owls trilled with tongues of nightingale.

These were all lies, though they matched the time,
And brought me less than luck: her image
Warped in the weather, turned beldamish.
Then back came winter on me at a bound,
The pallid sky heaved with a moon-quake.

Dangerous it had been with love-notes
To serenade Queen Famine.
In tears I recomposed the former scene,
Let the snow lie, watched the moon rise, suffered the
     owls,
Paid homage to them of unevent.

DAWN BOMBARDMENT

Guns from the sea open against us:
The smoke rocks bodily in the casemate
And a yell of doom goes up.
We count and bless each new, heavy concussion—
Captives awaiting rescue.

Visiting angel of the wild-fire hair
Who in dream reassured us nightly
Where we lay fettered,
Laugh at us, as we wake—our faces
So tense with hope the tears run down.

THE WORMS OF HISTORY

On the eighth day God died; his bearded mouth
That had been shut so long flew open.
So Adam's too in a dismay like death—
But the world still rolled on around him,
Instinct with all those lesser powers of life
That God had groaned against but not annulled.

' All-excellent ', Adam had titled God,
And in his mourning now demeaned himself
As if all excellence, not God, had died;
Chose to be governed by those lesser powers,
More than inferior to excellence—
The worms astir in God's corrupt flesh.

God died, not excellence his name:
Excellence lived, but only was not God.
It was those lesser powers who played at God,
Bloated with Adam's deferential sighs
In mourning for expired divinity;
They reigned as royal monsters upon earth.

Adam grew lean, and wore perpetual black;
He made no reaching after excellence.
Eve gave him sorry comfort for his grief
With birth of sons, and mourning still he died.
Adam was buried in one grave with God
And the worms ranged and ravaged in between.

Into their white maws fell abundance
Of all things rotten.   They were greedy-nosed
To smell the taint out and go scavenging,
Yet over excellence held no domain.
Excellence lives; they are already dead—
The ages of a putrefying corpse.

THE BEAST

Beyond the Atlas roams a love-beast;
The aborigines harry it with darts.
Its flesh is esteemed, though of a fishy tang
Tainting the eater's mouth and lips.
Ourselves once, wandering in mid-wilderness
And by despair drawn to this diet,
Before the meal was over sat apart
Loathing each other's carrion company.

A WITHERING HERB

Ambition in the herb denied his root.
In dreams of the dark he whispered:
'O to be all flower, and to star the sky—
True brother to the moon, that stemless flower
Who long has cherished me!'

Disdained the happy sun of morning,
Held it gross rival to the sovereign moon—
Thus for ambition cast his cloak of leaves
Yet could not snap the stem, to float upward
And from his roots be free:
So withered staunchly.

THE SHOT

The curious heart plays with its fears:
To hurl a shot through the ship's planks,
Being assured that the green angry flood
Is charmed and dares not dance into the hold—
Nor first to sweep a lingering glance around
For land or shoal or cask adrift.
'So miracles are done; but madmen drown.'

O weary luxury of hypothesis—
For human nature, honest human nature
(Which the fear-pampered heart denies)
Knows its own miracle: not to go mad.
Will pitch the shot in fancy, hint the fact,
Will bore perhaps a meagre auger hole
But stanch the spurting with a tarred rag,
And will not drown, nor even ride the cask.

THE THIEVES

Lovers in the act dispense
With such meum-teum sense
As might warningly reveal
What they must not pick or steal,
And their nostrum is to say:
'I and you are both away.'

After, when they disentwine
You from me and yours from mine,
Neither can be certain who
Was that I whose mine was you.
To the act again they go
More completely not to know.

Theft is theft and raid is raid
Though reciprocally made.
Lovers, the conclusion is
Doubled sighs and jealousies
In a single heart that grieves
For lost honour among thieves.

177

LOLLOCKS

By sloth on sorrow fathered,
These dusty-featured Lollocks
Have their nativity in all disordered
Backs of cupboard drawers.

They play hide and seek
Among collars and novels
And empty medicine bottles,
And letters from abroad
That never will be answered.

Every sultry night
They plague little children,
Gurgling from the cistern,
Humming from the air,
Skewing up the bed-clothes,
Twitching the blind.

When the imbecile agèd
Are over-long in dying
And the nurse drowses,
Lollocks come skipping
Up the tattered stairs
And are nasty together
In the bed's shadow.

The signs of their presence
Are boils on the neck,
Dreams of vexation suddenly recalled
In the middle of the morning,
Languor after food.

178

Men cannot see them,
Men cannot hear them,
Do not believe in them—
But suffer the more,
Both in neck and belly.

Women can see them—
O those naughty wives
Who sit by the fireside
Munching bread and honey,
Watching them in mischief
From corners of their eyes,
Slily allowing them to lick
Honey-sticky fingers.

Sovereign against Lollocks
Are hard broom and soft broom,
To well comb the hair,
To well brush the shoe,
And to pay every debt
So soon as it's due.

TO SLEEP

The mind's eye sees as the heart mirrors:
Loving in part, I did not see you whole,
Grew flesh-enraged that I could not conjure
A whole you to attend my fever-fit
In the doubtful hour between a night and day
And be Sleep that had kept so long away.

Of you sometimes a hand, a brooch, a shoe
Wavered beside me, unarticulated—
As the vexed insomniac dream-forges;
And the words I chose for your voice to speak
Echoed my own voice with its dry creak.

Now that I love you, now that I recall
All scattered elements of will that swooped
By night as jealous dreams through windows
To circle above the beds like bats,
Or as dawn-birds flew blindly at the panes
In curiosity rattling out their brains—

Now that I love you, as not before,
Now you can be and say, as not before:
The mind clears and the heart true-mirrors you
Where at my side an early watch you keep
And all self-bruising heads loll into sleep.

DESPITE AND STILL

Have you not read
The words in my head,
And I made part
Of your own heart?
We have been such as draw
The losing straw—
You of your gentleness,
I of my rashness,
Both of despair—
Yet still might share
This happy will:
To love despite and still.
Never let us deny
The thing's necessity,
But, O, refuse
To choose
Where chance may seem to give
Loves in alternative.

THE SUICIDE IN THE COPSE

The suicide, far from content,
Stared down at his own shattered skull:
Was this what he meant?

Had not his purpose been
To liberate himself from duns and dolts
By a change of scene?

From somewhere came a roll of laughter:
He had looked so on his wedding-day,
And the day after.

There was nowhere at all to go,
And no diversion now but to peruse
What literature the winds might blow

Into the copse where his body lay:
A year-old sheet of sporting news,
A crumpled schoolboy essay.

FRIGHTENED MEN

We were not ever of their feline race,
Never had hidden claws so sharp as theirs
In any half-remembered incarnation;
Have only the least knowledge of their minds
Through a grace on their part in thinking aloud;
And we remain mouse-quiet when they begin
Suddenly in their unpredictable way
To weave an allegory of their lives,
Making each point by walking round it—
Then off again, as interest is warmed.
What have they said? Or unsaid? What?
We understood the general drift only.

They are punctilious as implacable,
Most neighbourly to those who love them least.
A shout will scare them. When they spring, they
    seize.
The worst is when they hide from us and change
To something altogether other:
We meet them at the door, as who returns
After a one-hour-seeming century
To a house not his own.

A STRANGER AT THE PARTY

For annoyance, not shame,
  Under their covert stares
She would not give her name
  Nor demand theirs.

Soon everyone at the party,
  Who knew everyone,
Eyed her with plain envy
  For knowing none—

Such neighbourly mistrust
  Breathed across the floor,
Such familiar disgust
  With what they were and wore—

Until, as she was leaving,
  Her time out-stayed,
They tried to say they loved her;
  But pride forbade.

THE OATH

The doubt and the passion
Falling away from them,
   In that instant both
Take timely courage
From the sky's clearness
   To confirm an oath.

Her loves are his loves,
His trust is her trust;
   Else all were grief
And they, lost ciphers
On a yellowing page,
   Death overleaf.

Rumour of old battle
Growls across the air;
   Then let it growl
With no more terror
Than the creaking stair
   Or the calling owl.

She knows, as he knows,
Of a faithful-always
   And an always-dear
By early emblems
Prognosticated,
   Fulfilled here.

LANGUAGE OF THE SEASONS

Living among orchards, we are ruled
By the four seasons necessarily:
This from unseasonable frosts we learn
Or from usurping suns and haggard flowers—
Legitimist our disapproval.

Weather we knew, not seasons, in the city
Where, seasonless, orange and orchid shone,
Knew it by heavy overcoat or light,
Framed love in later terminologies
Than here, where we report how weight of snow,
Or weight of fruit, tears branches from the tree.

MID-WINTER WAKING

Stirring suddenly from long hibernation
I knew myself once more a poet
Guarded by timeless principalities
Against the worm of death, this hillside haunting;
And presently dared open both my eyes.

O gracious, lofty, shone against from under,
Back-of-the-mind-far clouds like towers;
And you, sudden warm airs that blow
Before the expected season of new blossom,
While sheep still gnaw at roots and lambless go—

Be witness that on waking, this mid-winter,
I found her hand in mine laid closely
Who shall watch out the Spring with me.
We stared in silence all around us
But found no winter anywhere to see.

THE ROCK AT THE CORNER

The quarrymen left ragged
A rock at the corner;
But over it move now
The comforting fingers
Of ivy and briar.

Nor will it need assurance
Of nature's compassion
When presently it weathers
To a noble landmark
Of such countenance

That travellers in winter
Will know it for a creature
On guard at the corner
Where deep snows ingratiate
The comforts of death.

THE BEACH

Louder than gulls the little children scream
Whom fathers haul into the jovial foam,
But others fearlessly rush in, breast high,
Laughing the salty water from their mouths——
Heroes of the nursery.

The horny boatman, who has seen whales
And flying fishes, who has sailed as far
As Demerara and the Ivory Coast,
Will warn them, when they crowd to hear his tales,
That every ocean smells alike of tar.

THE VILLAGERS AND DEATH

The Rector's pallid neighbour at The Firs,
Death, did not flurry the parishioners.
Yet from a weight of supersitious fears
Each tried to lengthen his own term of years.
He was congratulated who combined
Toughness of flesh and weakness of the mind
In consequential rosiness of face.
This dull and not ill-mannered populace
Pulled off their caps to Death, as they slouched by,
But rumoured him both atheist and spy.
All vowed to outlast him (though none ever did)
And hear the earth drum on his coffin-lid.
Their groans and whispers down the village street
Soon soured his nature, which was never sweet.

THE DOOR

When she came suddenly in
It seemed the door could never close again,
Nor even did she close it—she, she—
The room lay open to a visiting sea
That no door could restrain.

Yet when at last she smiled, tilting her head
To take her leave of me,
Where she had smiled, instead
There was a dark door closing endlessly,
The waves receded.

UNDER THE POT

Sulkily the sticks burn, and though they crackle
  With scorn under the bubbling pot, or spout
Magnanimous jets of flame against the smoke
  At each heel end a dirty sap breaks out.

Confess, creatures, how sulkily ourselves
  We hiss with doom, fuel of a sodden age—
Not rapt up roaring to the chimney stack
  On incandescent clouds of spirit or rage.

THROUGH NIGHTMARE

Never be disenchanted of
That place you sometimes dream yourself into,
Lying at large remove beyond all dream,
Or those you find there, though but seldom
In their company seated—

The untameable, the live, the gentle.
Have you not known them? Whom? They carry
Time looped so river-wise about their house
There's no way in by history's road
To name or number them.

In your sleepy eyes I read the journey
Of which disjointedly you tell; which stirs
My loving admiration, that you should travel
Through nightmare to a lost and moated land,
Who are timorous by nature.

TO LUCIA AT BIRTH

Though the moon beaming matronly and bland
  Greets you, among the crowd of the new-born,
With 'welcome to the world' yet understand
  That still her pale, lascivious unicorn
And bloody lion are loose on either hand:
  With din of bones and tantarará of horn
Their fanciful cortège parades the land—
  Pest on the high road, wild-fire in the corn.

Outrageous company to be born into,
  Lunatics of a royal age long dead.
Then reckon time by what you are or do,
  Not by the epochs of the war they spread.
  Hark how they roar; but never turn your head.
Nothing will change them, let them not change you.

DEATH BY DRUMS

If I cried out in anger against music,
   It was not that I cried
Against the pure and wholesome arsenic
   Necessary for suicide:
For suicide in the drums' racking riot
   Where horned moriscoes wailing to their bride
Scare every Lydian songster from the spot.

SHE TELLS HER LOVE WHILE HALF ASLEEP

She tells her love while half asleep,
In the dark hours,
With half-words whispered low:
As Earth stirs in her winter sleep
And puts out grass and flowers
Despite the snow,
Despite the falling snow.

THESEUS AND ARIADNE

High on his figured couch beyond the waves
He dreams, in dream recalling her set walk
Down paths of oyster-shell bordered with flowers
And down the shadowy turf beneath the vine.
He sighs: 'Deep sunk in my erroneous past
She haunts the ruins and the ravaged lawns.'

Yet still unharmed it stands, the regal house
Crooked with age and overtopped by pines
Where first he wearied of her constancy.
And with a surer foot she goes than when
Dread of his hate was thunder in the air,
When the pines agonized with flaws of wind
And flowers glared up at her with frantic eyes.
Of him, now all is done, she never dreams
But calls a living blessing down upon
What he would have mere rubble and rank grass;
Playing the queen to nobler company.

THE TWELVE DAYS OF CHRISTMAS

The impassioned child who stole the axe of power,
Debauched his virgin mother
And vowed in rage he would be God the Father,

Who, grown to strength, strangled her lion twins
And from a cloud, in chains,
Hung her with anvils at her ankle bones,

Who whipped her daughters with a bull's pizzle,
Forced them to take the veil
And heard their loveless prayers with a lewd smile—

Senile at last the way of all flesh goes:
Into the kitchen where roast goose,
Plum-pudding and mince-pies his red robes grease.

She from the tree-top, true to her deserts,
With wand and silver skirts
Presides unravished over all pure hearts.

THREE SHORT POEMS

Cold Weather Proverb

Fearless approach and puffed feather
In birds, famine bespeak;
In man, belly filled full.

To Poets under Pisces

Until the passing years establish
Aquarius who with fruitful spate
All dried pools will at last replenish,
Resign yourselves to celebrate,
Poets, with grief or hate,
These gasping rainbowed flurries of the Fish.

June

June, the jolly season of most bloodshed:
Soldiers with roses in their rifle barrels
And children, cherries bobbing at their ears,
Who roar them on like furious adjutants
Where the broad oak its feathered bonnet rears.

1805

At Viscount Nelson's lavish funeral,
    While the mob milled and yelled about St. Paul's,
A General chatted with an Admiral:

'One of your Colleagues, Sir, remarked today
    That Nelson's *exit*, though to be lamented,
Falls not inopportunely, in its way.'

'He was a thorn in our flesh,' came the reply—
    'The most bird-witted, unaccountable,
Odd little runt that ever I did spy.

'One arm, one peeper, vain as Pretty Poll,
    A meddler, too, in foreign politics
And gave his heart in pawn to a plain moll.

'He would dare lecture us Sea Lords, and then
    Would treat his ratings as though men of honour
And play at leap-frog with his midshipmen!

'We tried to box him down, but up he popped,
    And when he'd banged Napoleon at the Nile
Became too much the hero to be dropped.

'You've heard that Copenhagen "blind eye" story?
    We'd tied him to Nurse Parker's apron-strings—
By G–d, he snipped them through and snatched the
        glory!'

'Yet,' cried the General, 'six-and-twenty sail
    Captured or sunk by him off Tráfalgár—
That writes a handsome *finis* to the tale.'

'Handsome enough.   The seas are England's now.
That fellow's foibles need no longer plague us.
He died most creditably, I'll allow.'

'And, Sir, the secret of his victories?'
  'By his unServicelike, familiar ways, Sir,
He made the whole Fleet love him, damn his eyes!'

AT THE SAVOY CHAPEL

[From *World's Press News*, 22 Feb. 1945. 'Alexander Clifford, the war correspondent, is today marrying Flight Officer Jenny Nicholson, daughter of Robert Graves. They met in the front line.']

Up to the wedding, formal with heir-loom lace,
Press-cameras, carnations out of season,
Well-mellowed priest and well-trained choristers,

The relatives come marching, such as meet
Only at weddings and at funerals,
The elder generation with the eldest.

Family features for years undecided
What look to wear against a loveless world
Fix, as the wind veers, in the same grimace.

Each eyes the others with a furtive pity:
'Heavens, how she has aged—and he,
Grey hair and sunken cheeks, what a changed man!'

They stare wistfully at the bride (released
From brass buttons and the absurd salute)
In long white gown, bouquet and woman's pride.

'How suitable!' they whisper, and the whisper
'How suitable!' rustles from pew to pew;
To which I nod suitably grave assent.

Now for you, loving ones, who kneel at the altar
And preside afterwards at table—
The trophy sword that shears the cake recalling

202

What god you entertained last year together,
His bull neck looped with guts,
Trampling corpse-carpet through the villages—

Here is my private blessing: so to remain
As today you are, with features
Resolute and unchangeably your own.

THE LAST DAY OF LEAVE (1916)

We five looked out over the moor
At rough hills blurred with haze, and a still sea:
Our tragic day, bountiful from the first.

We would spend it by the lily lake
(High in a fold beyond the farthest ridge),
Following the cart-track till it faded out.

The time of berries and bell-heather;
Yet all that morning nobody went by
But shepherds and one old man carting turfs.

We were in love: he with her, she with him,
And I, the youngest one, the odd man out,
As deep in love with a yet nameless muse.

No cloud; larks and heath-butterflies,
And herons undisturbed fishing the streams;
A slow cool breeze that hardly stirred the grass.

When we hurried down the rocky slope,
A flock of ewes galloping off in terror,
There shone the waterlilies, yellow and white.

Deep water and a shelving bank.
Off went our clothes and in we went, all five,
Diving like trout between the lily groves.

The basket had been nobly filled:
Wine and fresh rolls, chicken and pineapple—
Our braggadocio under threat of war.

The fire on which we boiled our kettle
We fed with ling and rotten blackthorn root;
And the coffee tasted memorably of peat.

Two of us might stray off together
But never less than three kept by the fire,
Focus of our uncertain destinies.

We spoke little, our minds in tune—
A sigh or laugh would settle any theme;
The sun so hot it made the rocks quiver.

But when it rolled down level with us,
Four pairs of eyes sought mine as if appealing
For a blind-fate-aversive afterword:—

'Do you remember the lily lake?
We were all there, all five of us in love,
No one yet killed, widowed or broken-hearted.'

TO BE NAMED A BEAR

Bears gash the forest trees
    To mark the bounds
    Of their own hunting grounds;
They follow the wild bees
    Point by point home
    For love of honeycomb;
They browse on blueberries.

Then should I stare
If I am named a bear,
And is it not the truth?
Unkempt and surly with a sweet tooth
I tilt my muzzle toward the starry hub
Where Queen Callisto guards her cub,

But envy those that here
    All winter breathing slow
    Sleep warm under the snow,
That yawn awake when the skies clear,
    And lank with longing grow
No more than one brief month a year.

VII

DREAM OF A CLIMBER

Watch how this climber raises his own ladder
From earth to heaven, and not in a night
Nor from the secret, stony pillow.
(World patents pending; tested in the shops.)

Here's quality timber, nosings of pure brass,
The perfect phallo-spiritual tilt,
A fuzzy puff of cloud on top—
Excellent lure for angels and archangels!

Come, climber, with your scientific hat
And beady gambler's eye, ascend!
He pauses, poses for his camera-man:
'Well-known Climber About to Ascend.'

But in the published print, we may be sure,
He will appear, not on the lowest rung
But nearly out of view, almost in the cloud,
Leaning aside for an angel to pass,
His muscular broad hands a-glint in the sun,
And crampons on his feet.

THE PERSIAN VERSION

Truth-loving Persians do not dwell upon
The trivial skirmish fought near Marathon.
As for the Greek theatrical tradition
Which represents that summer's expedition
Not as a mere reconnaissance in force
By three brigades of foot and one of horse
(Their left flank covered by some obsolete
Light craft detached from the main Persian fleet)
But as a grandiose, ill-starred attempt
To conquer Greece—they treat it with contempt;
And only incidentally refute
Major Greek claims, by stressing what repute
The Persian monarch and the Persian nation
Won by this salutary demonstration:
Despite a strong defence and adverse weather
All arms combined magnificently together.

THE WEATHER OF OLYMPUS

Zeus was once overheard to shout at Hera:
　'You hate it, do you?　Well, I hate it worse—
East wind in May, sirocco all the Summer.
　Hell take this whole impossible Universe!'

A scholiast explains this warm rejoinder,
　Which sounds too man-like for Olympic use,
By noting that the snake-tailed chthonian winds
　Were answerable to Fate alone, not Zeus.

APOLLO OF THE PHYSIOLOGISTS

Despite this learned cult's official
And seemingly sincere denial
That they either reject or postulate
God, or God's scientific surrogate,
Prints of a deity occur *passim*
Throughout their extant literature. They make him
A dumb, dead-pan Apollo with a profile
Drawn in Victorian-Hellenistic style—
The pallid, bald, partitioned head suggesting
Wholly abstract cerebral functioning;
Or nude and at full length, this deity
Displays digestive, venous, respiratory
And nervous systems painted in bold colour
On his immaculate exterior.
Sometimes, *in verso*, a bald, naked Muse,
His consort, flaunts her arteries and sinews,
While, upside-down, crouched in her chaste abdomen,
Adored by men and wondered at by women,
Hangs a Victorian-Hellenistic foetus—
Fruit of her academic god's afflatus.

THE OLDEST SOLDIER

The sun shines warm on seven old soldiers
    Paraded in a row,
Perched like starlings on the railings—
    Give them plug-tobacco!

They'll croon you the Oldest-Soldier Song:
    Of Harry who took a holiday
From the sweat of ever thinking for himself
    Or going his own bloody way.

It was arms-drill, guard and kit-inspection,
    Like dreams of a long train-journey,
And the barrack-bed that Harry dossed on
    Went rockabye, rockabye, rockabye.

Harry kept his rifle and brasses clean,
    But Jesus Christ, what a liar!
He won the Military Medal
    For his coolness under fire.

He was never the last on parade
    Nor the first to volunteer,
And when Harry rose to be storeman
    He seldom had to pay for his beer.

Twenty-one years, and out Harry came
    To be odd-job man, or janitor,
Or commissionaire at a picture-house,
    Or, some say, bully to a whore.

But his King and Country calling Harry,
  He reported again at the Depôt,
To perch on this railing like a starling,
  The oldest soldier of the row.

GROTESQUES

i

My Chinese uncle, gouty, deaf, half-blinded,
And more than a trifle absent-minded,
Astonished all St. James's Square one day
By giving long and unexceptionably exact directions
To a little coolie girl, who'd lost her way.

ii

The Lion-faced Boy at the Fair
And the Heir Apparent
Were equally slow at remembering people's faces.
But whenever they met, incognito, in the Brazilian
Pavilion, the Row and such-like places,
They exchanged, it is said, their sternest nods—
Like gods of dissimilar races.

iii

Dr. Newman with the crooked pince-nez
Had studied in Vienna and Chicago.
Chess was his only relaxation.
And Dr. Newman remained unperturbed
By every nastier manifestation
Of plutodemocratic civilization:
All that was cranky, corny, ill-behaved,
Unnecessary, askew or orgiastic
Would creep unbidden to his side-door (hidden
Behind a poster in the Tube Station,
Nearly half-way up the moving-stairs),
Push its way in, to squat there undisturbed
Among box-files and tubular steel-chairs.

215

He was once seen at the Philharmonic Hall
Noting the reactions of two patients,
With pronounced paranoiac tendencies,
To old Dutch music. He appeared to recall
A tin of lozenges in his breast-pocket,
Put his hand confidently in—
And drew out a black imp, or sooterkin,
Six inches long, with one ear upside-down,
Licking at a vanilla ice-cream cornet—
Then put it back again with a slight frown.

iv

A Royal Duke, with no campaigning medals
To dignify his Orders, he would speak
Nostalgically at times of Mozambique
Where once the ship he cruised in ran aground:
How he drank cocoa, from a sailor's mug,
Poured from the common jug,
While loyal toasts went round.

v

Sir John addressed the Snake God in his temple,
Which was full of bats, not as a votary
But with the somewhat cynical courtesy,
Just short of condescension,
He might have paid the Governor-General
Of a small, hot, backward colony.
He was well versed in primitive religion,
But found this an embarrassing occasion:
The God was immense, noisy and affable,
Began to tickle him with a nervous chuckle,
Unfobbed a great gold clock for him to listen,
Hissed like a snake, and swallowed him at one mouthful.

216

THE EUGENIST

Come, human dogs, interfertilitate—
  Blackfellow and white lord, brown, yellow and red!
Accept the challenge of the lately bred
  Newfoundland terrier with the dachshund gait.[1]

Breed me gigantic pygmies, meek-eyed Scots,
  Phlegmatic Irish, perfume-hating Poles,
Poker-faced, toothy, pigtailed Hottentots,
  And Germans with no envy in their souls.

[1] *See :* Charles R. Stockard and collaborators : *The genetic and endocrinic basis for differences in form and behaviour, as elucidated by studies of contrasted pure-line dogbreeds and their hybrids.* (Philadelphia, 1941.)

A CIVIL SERVANT

While in this cavernous place employed
  Not once was I aware
Of my officious other-self
  Poised high above me there,

My self reversed, my rage-less part,
  A slimy yellowish cone—
Drip, drip; drip, drip—so down the years
  I stalagmized in stone.

Now pilgrims to the cave, who come
  To chip off what they can,
Prod me with child-like merriment:
  'Look, look! It's like a man!'

GULLS AND MEN

The naturalists of the Bass Rock
  On this vexatious point agree:
That sea-birds of all sorts that flock
  About the Bass, repeatedly
    Collide in mid-flight,

And neither by design, in play,
  Nor by design in shrewd assault,
But (as these patient watchers say,
  Eyes that are seldom proved at fault)
    By lack of foresight.

Stupidity, which poor and rich
  Hold the recognizance of man,
Precious stupidity, of which
  Let him denude himself who can
    And stand at God's height—

Stupidity that brings to birth
  More, always more, than to the grave,
The burden of all songs on earth,
  And by which men are brave
    And women contrite—

This jewel bandied from a cliff
  By gulls and razor-bills and such!
Where is man's vindication if
  Perfectibility's as much
    Bird-right as man-right?

TO JUAN AT THE WINTER SOLSTICE

There is one story and one story only
That will prove worth your telling,
Whether as learned bard or gifted child;
To it all lines or lesser gauds belong
That startle with their shining
Such common stories as they stray into.

Is it of trees you tell, their months and virtues,
Of strange beasts that beset you,
Of birds that croak at you the Triple will?
Or of the Zodiac and how slow it turns
Below the Boreal Crown,
Prison of all true kings that ever reigned?

Water to water, ark again to ark,
From woman back to woman:
So each new victim treads unfalteringly
The never altered circuit of his fate,
Bringing twelve peers as witness
Both to his starry rise and starry fall.

Or is it of the Virgin's silver beauty,
All fish below the thighs?
She in her left hand bears a leafy quince;
When, with her right she crooks a finger smiling,
How may the King hold back?
Royally then he barters life for love.

Or of the undying snake from chaos hatched,
Whose coils contain the ocean,
Into whose chops with naked sword he springs,
Then in black water, tangled by the reeds,
Battles three days and nights,
To be spewed up beside her scalloped shore?

Much snow is falling, winds roar hollowly,
The owl hoots from the elder,
Fear in your heart cries to the loving-cup:
Sorrow to sorrow as the sparks fly upward.
The log groans and confesses
There is one story and one story only.

Dwell on her graciousness, dwell on her smiling,
Do not forget what flowers
The great boar trampled down in ivy time.
Her brow was creamy as the crested wave,
Her sea-blue eyes were wild
But nothing promised that is not performed.

THE ALLANSFORD PURSUIT

[As danced by North-country witches at their Sabbaths. A restoration of the fragmentary seventeenth-century text.]

Cunning and art he did not lack
But aye her whistle would fetch him back.

O, I shall go into a hare
With sorrow and sighing and mickle care,
And I shall go in the Devil's name
Aye, till I be fetchèd hame.
    —Hare, take heed of a bitch greyhound
    Will harry thee all these fells around,
    For here come I in Our Lady's name
    All but for to fetch thee hame.

Cunning and art, etc.

Yet, I shall go into a trout
With sorrow and sighing and mickle doubt,
And show thee many a crooked game
Ere that I be fetchèd hame.
    —Trout, take heed of an otter lank
    Will harry thee close from bank to bank,
    For here come I in Our Lady's name
    All but for to fetch thee hame.

Cunning and art, etc.

Yet I shall go into a bee
With mickle horror and dread of thee
And flit to hive in the Devil's name
Ere that I be fetchèd hame.

—Bee, take heed of a swallow hen
Will harry thee close, both butt and ben,
For here come I in Our Lady's name
All but for to fetch thee hame.

Cunning and art, etc.

Yet I shall go into a mouse
And haste me unto the miller's house,
There in his corn to have good game
Ere that I be fetchèd hame.
    —Mouse, take heed of a white tib-cat
    That never was baulked of mouse or rat,
    For I'll crack thy bones in Our Lady's name:
    Thus shalt thou be fetchèd hame.

Cunning and art, etc.

THE ALPHABET CALENDAR OF AMERGIN

[The text restored from mediaeval Irish and Welsh variants.]

I am a stag: *of seven tines,*
I am a flood: *across a plain,*
I am a wind: *on a deep lake,*
I am a tear: *the Sun lets fall,*
I am a hawk: *above the cliff,*
I am a thorn: *beneath the nail,*
I am a wonder: *among flowers,*
I am a wizard: *who but I*
Sets the cool head aflame with smoke?

I am a spear: *that rears for blood,*
I am a salmon: *in a pool,*
I am a lure: *from paradise,*
I am a hill: *where poets walk,*
I am a boar: *ruthless and red,*
I am a breaker: *threatening doom,*
I am a tide: *that drags to death,*
I am an infant: *who but I*
Peeps from the unhewn dolmen arch?

I am the womb: *of every holt,*
I am the blaze: *on every hill,*
I am the queen: *of every hive,*
I am the shield: *for every head,*
I am the grave: *of every hope.*

THE SIREN'S WELCOME TO CRONOS

Cronos Odysseus, steer your boat
Toward Silver Island whence we sing;
Here you shall pass your days.

Through a thick-growing alder-wood
We clearly see, but are not seen,
Hid in a golden haze.

Our hair the hue of barley sheaf,
Our eyes the hue of blackbird's egg,
Our cheeks like asphodel.

Here the wild apple blossoms yet;
Wrens in the silver branches play
And prophesy you well.

Here nothing ill or harsh is found.
Cronos Odysseus, steer your boat
Across these placid straits,

With each of us in turn to lie
Taking your pleasure on young grass
That for your coming waits.

No grief nor gloom, sickness nor death,
Disturbs our long tranquillity;
No treachery, no greed.

Compared with this, what are the plains
Of Elis, where you ruled as king?
A wilderness indeed.

A starry crown awaits your head,
A hero feast is spread for you:
Swineflesh, milk and mead.

DICHETAL DO CHENNAIB

'Today it is by the finger ends that the poet effects the *Dichetal do chennaib*, and this is the way he does it. When he sees the required person or object before him he at once makes a poem with his finger tips, or in his mind without reflexion, composing and repeating simultaneously.'

(Mediaeval Irish scholiast on the *Senchus Mor*.)

Tree powers, finger tips,
First pentad of the four,
Discover all your poet asks
Drumming on his brow.

Birch-peg, throbbing thumb,
By power of divination,
Birch, bring him news of love;
Loud knocks the heart.

Rowan-rod, forefinger,
By power of divination,
Unriddle him a riddle;
The key's cast away.

Ash, middle finger,
By power of divination
Weather-wise, fool otherwise,
Mete him out the winds.

Alder, physic finger,
By power of divination
Diagnose all maladies
Of a doubtful mind.

Willow-wand, earfinger,
By power of divination
Force confessions from the mouth
Of a mouldering corpse.

Finger-ends, five twigs,
Trees, true-divining trees,
Discover all your poet asks
Drumming on his brow.

THE BATTLE OF THE TREES

[Text reassembled and restored from the deliberately confused mediaeval Welsh poem-medley, *Câd Goddeu*, in the *Red
Book of Hergest*, hitherto regarded as nonsensical.]

The tops of the beech tree
Have sprouted of late,
Are changed and renewed
From their withered state.

When the beech prospers,
Though spells and litanies
The oak tops entangle,
There is hope for trees.

I have plundered the fern,
Through all secrets I spy,
Old Math ap Mathonwy
Knew no more than I.

For with nine sorts of faculty
God has gifted me:
I am fruit of fruits gathered
From nine sorts of tree—

Plum, quince, whortle, mulberry,
Raspberry, pear,
Black cherry and white
With the sorb in me share.

From my seat at Fefynedd,
A city that is strong,
I watched the trees and green things
Hastening along.

228

Retreating from happiness
    They would fain be set
In forms of the chief letters
    Of the alphabet.

Wayfarers wondered,
    Warriors were dismayed
At renewal of conflicts
    Such as Gwydion made,

At a battle raging
    Under each tongue root
Of a hundred-headed thing,
    A monstrous brute,

A toad with a hundred claws
    Armed at his thighs;
And in his head-recesses
    Raging likewise.

The alders in the front line
    Began the affray.
Willow and rowan-tree
    Were tardy in array.

The holly, dark green,
    Made a resolute stand;
He is armed with many spear points
    Wounding the hand.

With foot-beat of the swift oak
    Heaven and earth rung;
'Stout Guardian of the Door,'
    His name in every tongue.

Great was the gorse in battle,
    And the ivy at his prime;
The hazel was arbiter
    At this charmed time.

Uncouth and savage was the fir,
    Cruel the ash-tree—
Turns not aside a foot-breadth,
    Straight at the heart runs he.

The birch, though very noble,
    Armed himself but late:
A sign not of cowardice
    But of high estate.

The heath gave consolation
    To the toil-spent folk,
The long-enduring poplars
    In battle much broke.

Some of them were cast away
    On the field of fight
Because of holes torn in them
    By the enemy's might.

Very wrathful was the vine
    Whose henchmen are the elms;
I exalt him mightily
    To rulers of realms.

Strong chieftains were the blackthorn
    With his ill fruit,
The unbeloved whitethorn
    Who wears the same suit,

230

The swift-pursuing reed,
　The broom with his brood,
And the furze but ill-behaved
　Until he is subdued.

The dower-scattering yew
　Stood glum at the fight's fringe,
With the elder slow to burn
　Amid fires that singe,

And the blessed wild apple
　Laughing in pride
From the *Gorchan* of Maelderw
　By the rock side.

In shelter linger
　Privet and woodbine,
Inexperienced in warfare,
　And the courtly pine.

But I, although slighted
　Because I was not big,
Fought, trees, in your array
　On the field of Goddeu Brig.

THE SONG OF BLODEUWEDD

[Text reassembled and restored from the same poem-medley
as the foregoing.]

Not of father nor of mother
Was my blood, was my body.
I was spellbound by Gwydion,
Prime enchanter of the Britons,
When he formed me from nine blossoms,
 Nine buds of various kind:
From primrose of the mountain,
Broom, meadow-sweet and cockle,
 Together intertwined,
From the bean in its shade bearing
A white spectral army
 Of earth, of earthy kind,
From blossoms of the nettle,
Oak, thorn and bashful chestnut—
Nine powers of nine flowers,
 Nine powers in me combined,
 Nine buds of plant and tree.
Long and white are my fingers
 As the ninth wave of the sea.

INTERCESSION IN LATE OCTOBER

How hard the year dies: no frost yet.
On drifts of yellow sand Midas reclines,
Fearless of moaning reed or sullen wave.
Firm and fragrant still the brambleberries.
On ivy-bloom butterflies wag.

Spare him a little longer, Crone,
For his clean hands and love-submissive heart.

INSTRUCTIONS TO THE ORPHIC ADEPT

*[In part translated from the Timpone Grande and Campagno
Orphic tablets.]*

So soon as ever your mazed spirit descends
From daylight into darkness, Man, remember
What you have suffered here in Samothrace,
What you have suffered.

After your passage through Hell's seven floods,
Whose fumes of sulphur will have parched your throat,
The Halls of Judgement will loom up before you,
A miracle of jasper and of onyx.
To the left hand there bubbles a black spring
Overshadowed with a great white cypress.
Avoid this spring, which is Forgetfulness;
Though all the common rout rush down to drink,
Avoid this spring.

To the right hand there lies a secret pool
Alive with speckled trout and fish of gold;
A hazel overshadows it.   Ophion,
Primaeval serpent straggling in the branches,
Darts out his tongue.   This holy pool is fed
By dripping water; guardians stand before it.
Run to this pool, the pool of Memory,
Run to this pool.

Then will the guardians scrutinize you, saying:
'Who are you, who?   What have you to remember?
Do you not fear Ophion's flickering tongue?
Go rather to the spring beneath the cypress,
Flee from this pool.'

Then you shall answer: 'I am parched with thirst.
Give me to drink. I am a child of Earth,
But of Sky also, come from Samothrace.
Witness the glint of amber on my brow.
Out of the Pure I come, as you may see.
I also am of your thrice-blessed kin,
Child of the three-fold Queen of Samothrace;
Have made full quittance for my deeds of blood,
Have been by her invested in sea-purple,
And like a kid have fallen into milk,
Give me to drink, now I am parched with thirst,
Give me to drink!'

But they will ask you yet: 'What of your feet?'
You shall reply: 'My feet have borne me here
Out of the weary wheel, the circling years,
To that still, spokeless wheel:—Persephone.
Give me to drink!'

Then they will welcome you with fruit and flowers,
And lead you toward the ancient dripping hazel,
Crying: 'Brother of our immortal blood,
Drink and remember glorious Samothrace!'
Then you shall drink.

You shall drink deep of that refreshing draught,
To become lords of the uninitiated
Twittering ghosts, Hell's countless populace—
To become heroes, knights upon swift horses,
Pronouncing oracles from tall white tombs
By the nymphs tended. They with honey water
Shall pour libations to your serpent shapes,
That you may drink.

LAMENT FOR PASIPHAË

Dying sun, shine warm a little longer!
My eye, dazzled with tears, shall dazzle yours,
Conjuring you to shine and not to move.
You, sun, and I all afternoon have laboured
Beneath a dewless and oppressive cloud—
A fleece now gilded with our common grief
That this must be a night without a moon.
Dying sun, shine warm a little longer!

Faithless she was not: she was very woman,
Smiling with dire impartiality,
Sovereign, with heart unmatched, adored of men,
Until Spring's cuckoo with bedraggled plumes
Tempted her pity and her truth betrayed.
Then she who shone for all resigned her being,
And this must be a night without a moon.
Dying sun, shine warm a little longer!

THE TETRAGRAMMATON

[A magical gloss on Numbers vi, 23-27.]

Light was his first day of Creation,
Peace after labour was his seventh day,
Life and the Glory are his day of days.

He carved his law on tables of sapphirus,
Jerusalem shines with his pyrope gates,
Four cherubs fetch him amber from the north.

Acacia yields her timber for his ark,
Pomegranate sanctifies his priestly hem,
His hyssop sprinkles blood at every door.

Holy, Holy, Holy, is his name.

NUNS AND FISH

Circling the circlings of their fish
   Nuns walk in white and pray;
   For he is chaste as they,
   Who was dark-faced and hot in Silvia's day,
And in his pool drowns each unspoken wish.

THE DESTROYER

Swordsman of the narrow lips,
Narrow hips and murderous mind
Fenced with chariots and ships,
By your joculators hailed
The mailed wonder of mankind,
Far to westward you have sailed.

You it was dared seize the throne
Of a blown and amorous prince
Destined to the Moon alone,
A lame, golden-heeled decoy,
Joy of hens that gape and wince
Inarticulately coy.

You who, capped with lunar gold
Like an old and savage dunce,
Let the central hearth go cold,
Grinned, and left us here your sword
Warden of sick fields that once
Sprouted of their own accord.

Gusts of laughter the Moon stir
That her Bassarids now bed
With the ignoble usurer
While an ignorant pale priest
Rides the beast with a man's head
To her long-omitted feast.

RETURN OF THE GODDESS

Under your Milky Way
  And slow-revolving Bear
Frogs from the alder thicket pray
In terror of your judgement day,
  Loud with repentance there.

The log they crowned as king
  Grew sodden, lurched and sank;
An owl floats by on silent wing
Dark water bubbles from the spring;
  They invoke you from each bank.

At dawn you shall appear,
  A gaunt red-leggèd crane,
You whom they know too well for fear,
Lunging your beak down like a spear
  To fetch them home again.

Sufficiunt
Tecum,
Caryatis,
Domnia
Quina.

THE END